D0846308

Bloomfield Twp. Public Library
1099 Lone Pine Road
Bloomfield Hills, MI 48302-2410

Historical Atlases of South Asia,
Central Asia, and the Middle East ™

A HISTORICAL ATLAS OF

JORDAN

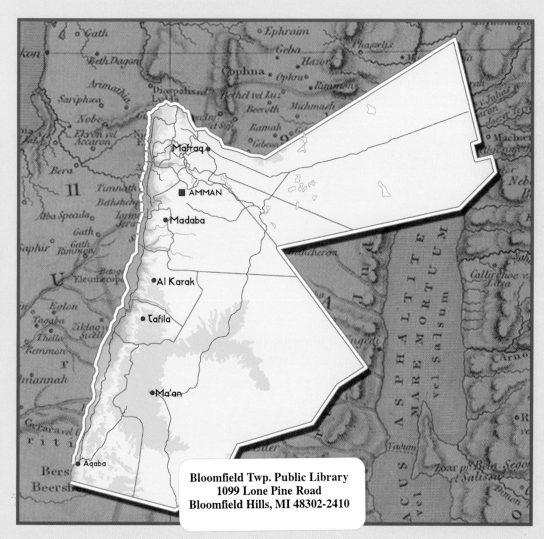

Bloomfield Twp. Public Library
1099 Lone Pine Road
Bloomfield Hills, MI 48302-2410

Amy Romano

The Rosen Publishing Group, Inc., New York

For my husband, Don, and my children, Claudia, Sam, and Jack

Published in 2004 by The Rosen Publishing Group, Inc.
29 East 21st Street, New York, NY 10010

Copyright © 2004 by The Rosen Publishing Group, Inc.

First Edition

All rights reserved. No part of this book may be reproduced in any form without permission in writing from the publisher, except by a reviewer.

Publisher Cataloging Data

Romano, Amy
A historical atlas of Jordan / Amy Romano.
     p. cm. — (Historical atlases of South Asia, Central Asia, and the Middle East)
Includes bibliographical references and index.
Summary: Maps and text chronicle the history of Jordan, a Middle Eastern country that became independent in 1946.
ISBN 0-8239-3980-4
1. Jordan—History—Maps for children 2. Jordan—Maps for children [1. Jordan—History 2. Atlases]
I. Title II. Series
911'.5695—dc21

Manufactured in the United States of America

Cover image: Jordan *(twenty-first century map, center)*, once a part of Palestine *(nineteenth-century map, background)*, has been affected by medieval rulers such as Saladin *(top left)* and shaped by modern leaders such as King Abdullah II *(bottom left)*. The floor mosaic *(right)*, a detail of the sixth-century Hall of Hyppolytus, is considered an artifact from biblical Jordan.

Contents

FEB 1 2 2004

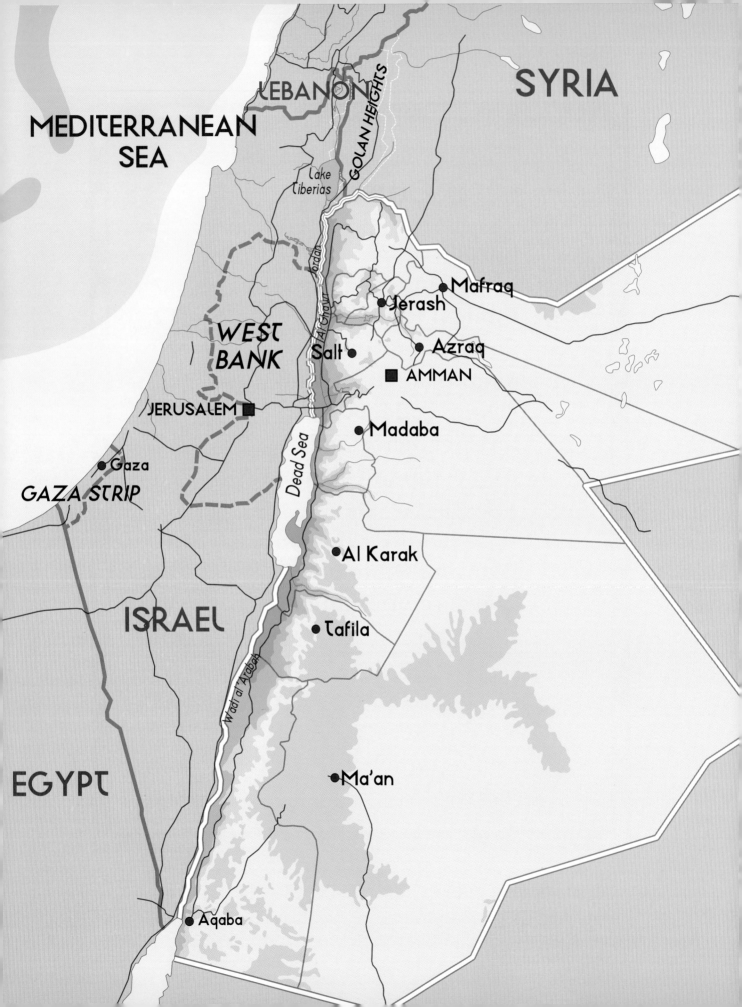

INTRODUCTION

SAUDI
ARABIA

Jordan, officially named the Hashemite Kingdom of Jordan, is a young nation molded by centuries of passing civilizations. Although the country did not gain independence until 1946, its age as a nation is dwarfed by the magnitude of its place in history.

Jordan was once home to some of the earliest recorded settlements, with archaeological evidence of organized civilizations dating back to 9000 BC. Jordan has hosted peoples of many of the world's greatest civilizations. Egyptians, Assyrians, Babylonians, Hittites, Greeks, Romans, and Turks have all found their way through the region, each leaving a permanent mark on its development.

Jordan also roughly corresponds to the biblical lands of Ammon, Bashan, Edom, Gilead, and Moab and is home to nearly one hundred recorded biblical sites. It is through Jordan that Abraham led the

King Hussein (1935–1999), who ruled Jordan soon after its independence in 1946, led the country through several wars and attempted coups. Under his leadership, Jordan has remained nearly self-sufficient, though it lacks the same oil-rich resources of many other Middle Eastern countries. For the last twenty years of his reign, Hussein pushed toward peaceful relations with all Arab nations. King Abdullah II, Hussein's son, became king upon his father's death in 1999. Today, Jordan remains a political ally of the United States as well as a home to many displaced Palestinians.

This photograph, taken by Robert Holmes in 1993, shows a Bedouin shepherd making his way across the Wadi Rum section of Jordan. Bedouin are Arab nomads who travel in clans throughout the Middle East in search of adequate water. The Jordanian government offers assistance to its Bedouin population, though few take advantage of state programs. Some have settled long enough to grow meager crops, though most have combined lifestyles of both settlement and travel. Bedouin, known for their hospitality, will never turn away a fellow traveler.

Israelites out of Egypt to their first sighting of the Promised Land; that Lot sought refuge from the destruction of Sodom and Gomorrah; and, in ancient Jordan, that Christ was born, baptized, and died.

Today's Jordan is a predominantly Arab nation, home to descendants of Bedouin (nomadic) tribes. Modern Jordanian men still lead herds of goats and sheep across its arid desert. Located in the Middle East between the Mediterranean Sea and the Arabian Peninsula, the country covers approximately 37,740 square miles (60,723 square kilometers) and is roughly the size of Indiana.

Jordan shares its northernmost border with Syria. Iraq lies to the northeast. Saudi Arabia, in the east and south, makes up Jordan's longest border. The territories most commonly referred to as Palestine— Israel and the West Bank—make up Jordan's western boundary. Finally, a mere 16.3 miles (26 kilometers) of coastline along the Red Sea in the southwest save Jordan from being completely landlocked.

Because of its central location, Jordan is often referred to as the crossroads of the Middle East. Throughout history, its neighboring countries have existed not simply as the meeting point for nations but as an area that connects both people and continents. Modern Jordan continues to maintain its vital position to this day.

1 JORDAN IN ANTIQUITY

Since the dawn of humankind, few sections of the land known today as Jordan have been able to support life. During prehistoric times, lands south and east of Jordan did not receive enough rainfall to support more than sparse nomadic tribes, or Bedouin. The long history of this region focuses on its fertile lands in the north and west.

The Stone Age

Archaeological finds indicate the presence of nomadic hunters in the region known as Jordan as far back as the Paleolithic era (40,000–12,000 BC). The most significant of these discoveries is located at the Azraq oasis in the country's eastern desert. During this period, Jordan's climate was that of a somewhat fertile savanna.

Further discoveries provide evidence of a changing lifestyle among inhabitants by the end of the Mesolithic era. Nomadic hunter-gatherers settled, building huts with underground foundations. They incorporated tools into their farming efforts, and they domesticated animals. These semipermanent communities are most notable in southern Jordan near the city of Bayda, near Petra in the Jordan Valley, and in Jericho in the West Bank.

This contemporary photograph of Jordan shows the remains of a Neolithic (7500–6700 BC) settlement. Its inhabitants likely lived in small houses made of stone and survived by eating crops of various grains, peas, and lentils. Historians and archaeologists have also proven that these Neolithic families raised livestock, worshiped in temples, buried their dead in underground tombs, and created sculptures of the human form.

During the Neolithic era, changes occurred that altered life in this region. Permanent villages such as Bayda and Ain Ghazal, northeast of Amman, were made up of many multiroomed houses, some even with finished flooring.

The next major shift resulted from changing weather. As temperatures began to rise, the once fertile eastern savanna became arid and uninhabitable. This evolution resulted in a population shift to the west.

By 3500 BC, inhabitants were smelting copper, along with using their older skills of making clay vessels. Subsequent excavations indicate the planned cultivation of crops as well as the breeding of sheep and goats.

The Bronze Age

Between 3200 and 1200 BC, or the period known as the Bronze Age, the tribal settlements of Jordan grew into small cities. A city known to archaeologists as Jawa is perhaps the earliest advanced settlement in Jordan, dating back to 4000 BC. Built in a desolate area known as the Black Desert, Jawa is believed to have once been a thriving community.

Other communities have been unearthed at the Citadel in present-day Amman. In the southern desert, Semitic tribes known as the Canaanites grew into a community. Semites are people who speak a Semitic language, such as Arabic or Hebrew. In addition to their engineering skills, the Canaanites were Jordan's earliest traders, often mixing with other communities.

Around 2300 BC, many of the towns in Jordan were destroyed. Controversy remains as to the cause of this destruction, citing either the Amorites—a newer Semitic people who may have come to power—or an

Palestine

Palestine is one of the world's most historic places. Located at the eastern end of the Mediterranean Sea between Egypt and southwest Asia, it is the birthplace of two of the world's greatest religions—Judaism and Christianity. Palestine is often referred to as the Holy Land, and it is the site of many religious events. Muslims, the followers of Islam, also consider Palestine to be sacred. The Dome of the Rock was built to commemorate the prophet Muhammad's famous night journey. He was transported from Mecca to Jerusalem in a mystical flight, and a shrine was later built on the rock from where he ascended to heaven. The second mosque in al-Haram al-Sharif, at the end of a walkway connecting it to the Dome of the Rock, is al-Aqsa Mosque, or the Farthest Mosque. It is so named in reference to the verse in the Koran citing Jerusalem as "the far distant place of worship."

Palestine's location has made it a center of conflict. Never an independent state, many of the greatest empires in history have invaded the region. In the four hundred years before World War I, Palestine was part of the Ottoman Empire. After the war, Palestine came under British control. Divided among Israel, Jordan, and Egypt after a series of wars, many of Palestine's Arab and Jewish residents became refugees. Conflicts over Palestine continue today.

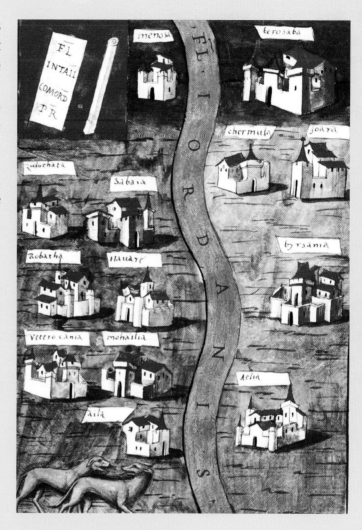

This medieval map of Palestine showing the Jordanian River Valley was created during the fifteenth century. Once a part of an illuminated manuscript, it illustrates the region under the control of the Mamluks, after it was freed from Christian crusaders in 1187. The Mamluk Empire ruled over Palestine until 1516. Next, Ottoman Turks from Asia Minor defeated the Mamluks and divided Palestine into separate districts. This map is now part of a collection in the National Library of Spain, located in Madrid.

earthquake. Trade continued despite the destruction, however, and by 2000 BC, goods were flowing through the region among Egypt, Arabia, and the city-states of Syria and Palestine.

Inhabitants also mixed copper with tin to create bronze, making durable weapons and tools. Other developments at this time included the formation of a syllabic script.

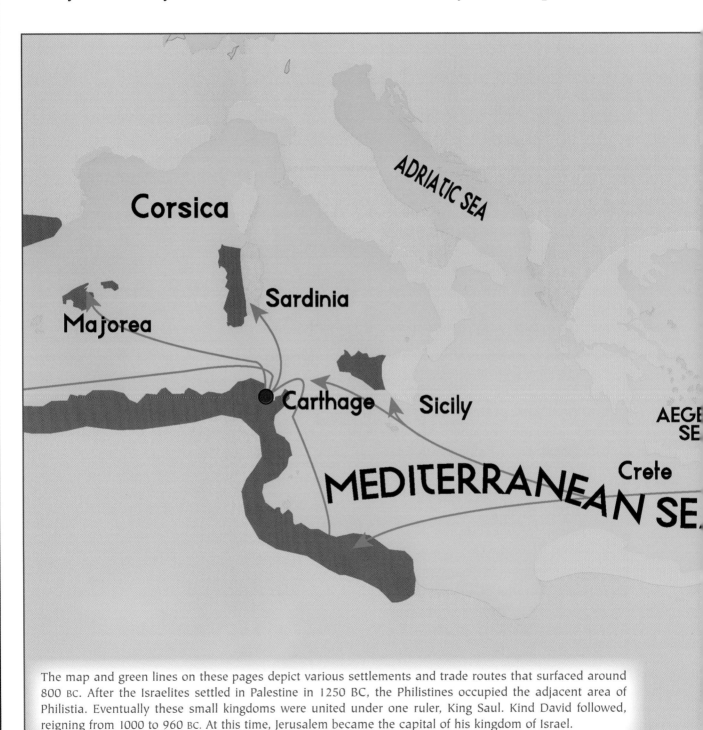

The map and green lines on these pages depict various settlements and trade routes that surfaced around 800 BC. After the Israelites settled in Palestine in 1250 BC, the Philistines occupied the adjacent area of Philistia. Eventually these small kingdoms were united under one ruler, King Saul. Kind David followed, reigning from 1000 to 960 BC. At this time, Jerusalem became the capital of his kingdom of Israel.

The destructive forces of the Hyksos—nomadic herders from central Asia who overran much of the territory—spoiled this prosperity. Around 1550 BC, Egyptians removed the Hyksos from Jordan to begin nearly three hundred years of peaceful influence. This period was brought to an end by the arrival of hostile invaders known as the Peoples of the Sea, or Philistines. An ancient people who settled along the coast of Canaan (Palestine), an area then known as the Plain of Philistia, the Philistines took control of Jordan and cities in Greece and Cyprus. As Philistine power grew, Egyptian forces left Jordan to fight them on their own land.

Philistine power would later be challenged in the eleventh century by the exodus (mass emigration) of tribes known as Israelites. According to history recounted in the Bible, the prophet Moses led this group out of Egypt and across Jordan to the Promised Land. After this exodus, the Philistines retreated. From this point forward, Jordan's history has largely been one of invasion and conquest.

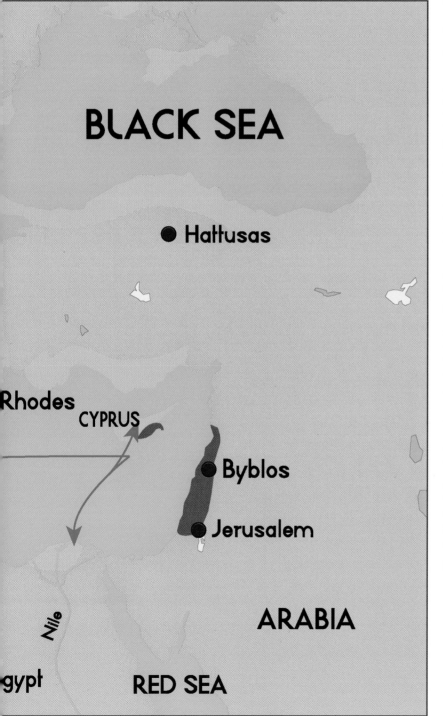

BLACK SEA

Hattusas

Rhodes

CYPRUS

Byblos

Jerusalem

Nile

Egypt

ARABIA

RED SEA

2 BIBLICAL JORDAN

Beginning around 1200 BC, the land later known as Jordan was divided into three kingdoms. The Edomites settled in the southern region; the Moabites, another Semitic tribe, settled near Wadi Mujib along the western border; and the Ammonites established a capital at Rabbath Ammon (Amman). A portion of this period in Jordanian history is detailed in the Bible through the stories of King David and his son Solomon.

The Rise of the Israelites

The years after 1200 BC saw the consolidation and development of these kingdoms (Ammon, Moab, and Edom) into trading centers. All three lay on the Arabian-Syrian trade route for precious metals and spices. This north–south route, known as the King's Highway, is one of three passages still in use today. Although business prospered, times

Abraham Ortelius (1528–1598) created this sixteenth-century map entitled "The Journey and Life of Abraham the Patriarch." Ortelius was a Flemish cartographer known for publishing the world's first atlas, *Theatrum Orbis Terrarum* or *Theatre of the World*. This map, created in 1590, depicts the land of Canaan and is surrounded by twenty-two small circles that chronicle Abraham's life. The inset map traces Abraham's route from Mesopotamia (present-day Iraq) to Shechem, Israel.

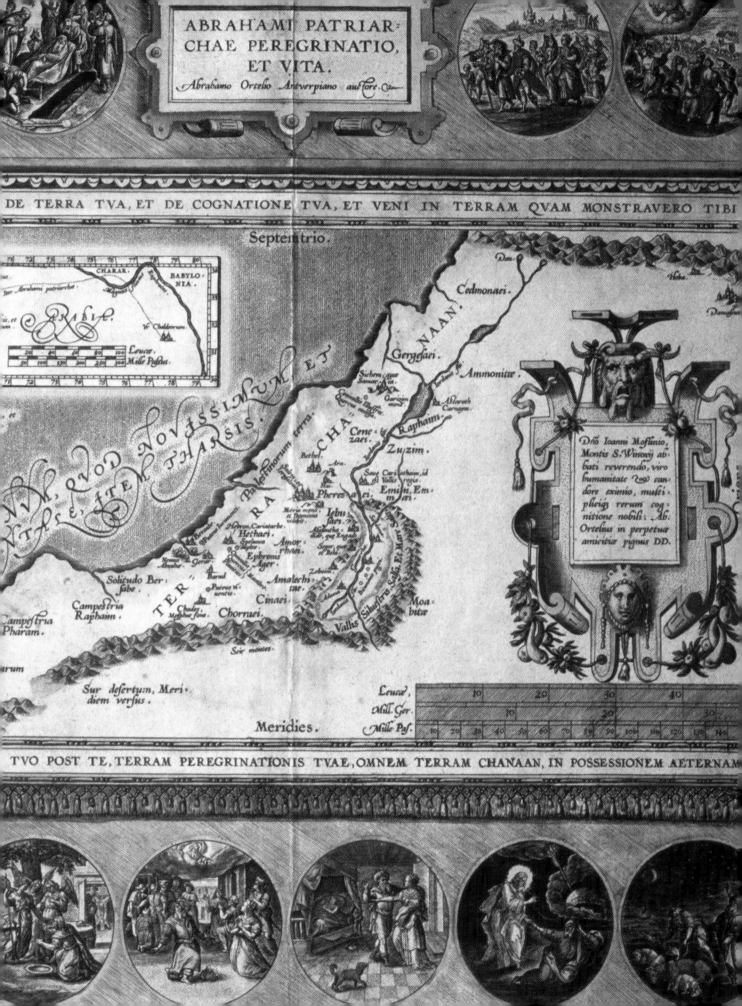

ABRAHAMI PATRIAR=
CHAE PEREGRINATIO,
ET VITA.

Abrahamo Ortelio Antwerpiano auctore.

DE TERRA TVA, ET DE COGNATIONE TVA, ET VENI IN TERRAM QVAM MONSTRAVERO TIBI

Septemtrio.

BABYLO-NIA.
CHARAR.

ARABIA.

Leucæ.
Mille Passus.

Dan.
Heba.

Cedmonæi.

NAAN

Gergesæi.

Ammonitæ.

Damascus

Sichem, quæ
Samaria

Garizim mons

Raphaim

Bethel

Cene zaei.

Zuzim.

Emim, Em mæi.

Pherefæi

Iebu saei.

Amor rhæi.

Hebron, Cariatarbe

Ephrons Ager

Amalechi tæ.

Campeftria
Raphaim.

Solicudo Ber fabe.

Cinæi.

Chorræi.

Moa bitæ

Vallis

Sir montes.

Sur defertum, Meri diem versus.

Meridies.

Leucæ.
Mill. Ger.
Mille Paf.

Dño Ioanni Moflinio, Montis S.Winox̄ij ab bati reverendo, viro humanitate & can dore eximio, multi plicig̃ rerum cog nitione nobili. Ab: Ortelius in perpetuæ amicitiæ pignus DD.

TVO POST TE, TERRAM PEREGRINATIONIS TVAE, OMNEM TERRAM CHANAAN, IN POSSESSIONEM AETERNAM

were anything but peaceful. The three tribes fought among themselves as well as against the ever-growing power of the Israelites for control.

By 1000 BC, the Israelites gained strength under the leadership of King David and declared a kingdom of Israel. David eventually expanded his kingdom to include the entire Levant. ("Levant" is a term that refers to the countries that lie on or near the eastern Mediterranean Sea.) The most notable of David's conquests was his defeat of the Ammonite king Uriah, the Hittite in Rabbath Ammon. Among the spoils of this victory was a wife for David, Uriah's wife, Bathsheba. David and Bathsheba had a son, Solomon, who would become king upon his father's death in 960 BC. Solomon ruled the Israelite Empire through a period of prosperity.

Israelite control would begin to falter after Solomon's death in 922 BC, and the region was divided. Israel, with its capital in Samaria, located north of present-day Jerusalem, would occupy the northern territory and Judah the south. The land known as Judah roughly corresponds to the region

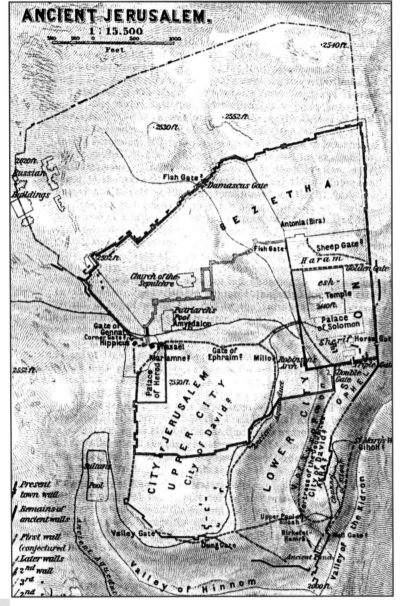

Taken from *Palestine and Syria: A Handbook for Travelers*, by Karl Baedeker, this historic map of ancient Jerusalem was published in 1912. It shows the city's various fortifications, the upper and lower divisions under King David, the Palace of Herod, and the Palace of Solomon. In the Christian Quarter, the Church of the Holy Sepulchre can be seen. This church, built on the "hill of the skull," is where the body of Jesus Christ was carried and entombed after he was crucified in AD 30.

in the southwest commonly referred to as Palestine. Jerusalem was established as Judah's capital.

Centuries of Changing Hands

In the early eighth century BC, an Assyrian army from Syria conquered both Damascus, the capital of Syria, and Israel. Judah and its major cities of Ammon, Edom, and Moab retained their independence.

One hundred years later, in 612 BC, Babylonian armies from Mesopotamia and the Medes from Persia defeated the Assyrians under the leadership of Babylon's King Nebuchadnezzar II (630–562 BC). Babylonian forces would rule the Levant for fifty years, severely limiting Jordan's independence. During Babylonian rule, both Jerusalem and Solomon's Temple on Mount Moriah were destroyed, and thousands of Israelites were deported to Babylon.

Cyrus II (died 530 BC), also known as Cyrus the Great, was the leader of the Babylonian defeat in 593 BC. He and his forces rebuilt Solomon's Temple and permitted the return of the Israelites to Judah. Although the Ammonites and the Moabites made attempts to oust Persian powers, they were unsuccessful. Two centuries passed under relatively stable Persian rule.

By 333 BC, Alexander the Great (356–323 BC), a Macedonian general, defeated the ruling Persian armies in Turkey and Egypt. Upon his death in Babylon in 323 BC, he controlled a huge empire that stretched from present-day Greece to India.

The Greeks and Nabateans

Alexander brought to the region Hellenistic (Greek) influences that lasted for three centuries. After his death, his generals Seleucus and Ptolemy divided the eastern part of his empire between them. Jordan, along with Palestine and southern Syria, went to Ptolemy. Because neither man was satisfied with the breadth of his empire, they battled for years to gain control of the other's territory. As a result, Jordan was caught in the crossfire.

While this conflict between Seleucus and Ptolemy raged, a nomadic tribe of Arabs known as the Nabateans established settlements around Edom. Upon their arrival in the sixth century BC, they established a capital in Petra and used its strategic position to gain wealth. Because of its ample water supply, Petra became a major stopping point on the caravan route from Arabia to the Mediterranean Sea. By the fourth century BC, the Nabataeans had become powerful

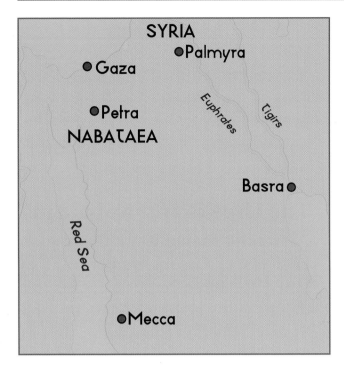

This map shows the extent of the Nabataean kingdom and its capital city, Petra, around the sixth century BC. The once nomadic Nabataeans created a trading empire in the region later known as Jordan by taxing traveling caravans on their way from Arabia to cities in the Mediterranean.

In 198 BC, the Seleucids finally defeated the Ptolomies and took control of Jordan, excluding the Nabataean territories in the south. With the Seleucid victory, trade again flourished.

At the same time, Jewish rebels under the leadership of Judas Maccabee were gaining power. These rebels invaded Jordan in 165 BC, sending the Seleucid Empire into a temporary, then terminal, decline. Less than a century later, Judas's successor would bring Jordan under Jewish control. Again, the Nabataean kingdom remained independent.

The Romans

In 64 BC, the Roman general Pompey became concerned about the growth of Nabataean power. Although unable to unseat Nabataean leaders from Petra, Pompey and his armies were able to conquer northern Jordan. During the relatively brief Jewish occupation, many of the northern cities—such as Gerasa,

enough to lead an unofficial empire in southern Jordan and would remain there for another six hundred years.

The contemporary photograph (left) shows excavated ruins in ancient Petra, a street of facades that lend their style to the influence of the Greeks and Romans. At the time of this writing, only a small percentage of Petra has been uncovered, including what archaeologists believe is a Great Temple. Petra was once home to more than 30,000 people between 200 BC and AD 100. This map (right) illustrates Herod's kingdom and the ten cities known as the Decapolis, Roman vassal city-states that paid taxes to the Romans under Pompey.

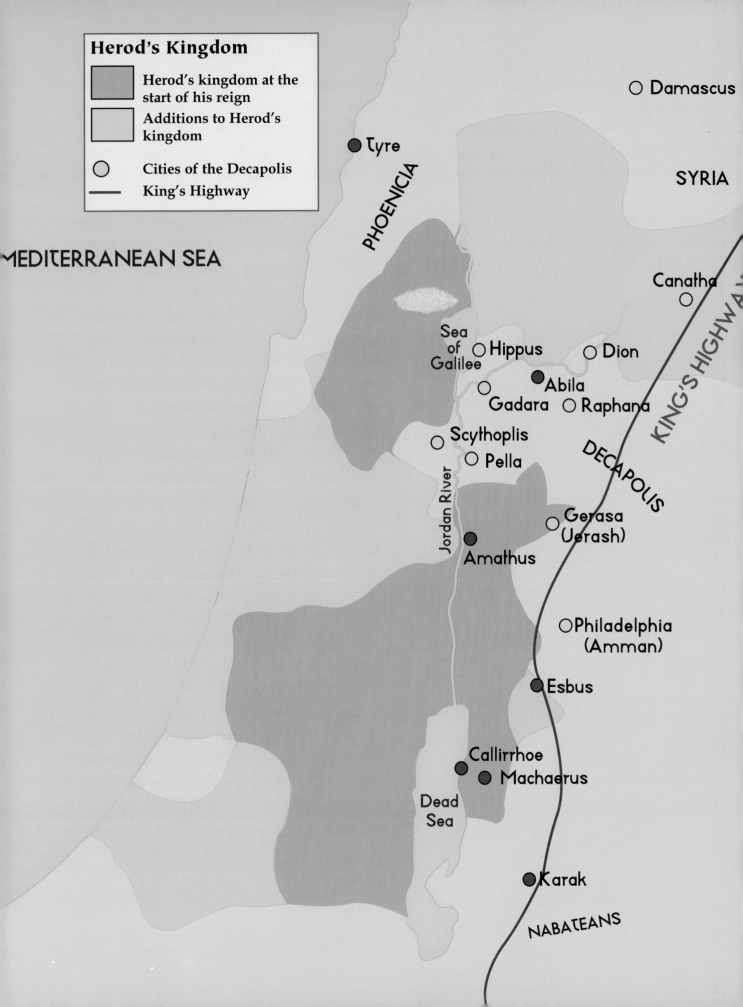

Herod's Kingdom

Herod's kingdom at the start of his reign

Additions to Herod's kingdom

○ Cities of the Decapolis

— King's Highway

MEDITERRANEAN SEA

PHOENICIA

SYRIA

○ Damascus

● Tyre

Canatha ○

Sea of Galilee

○ Hippus

○ Dion

● Abila

○ Gadara

○ Raphana

Scythoplis ○

DECAPOLIS

KING'S HIGHWAY

Pella ○

Jordan River

Gerasa (Jerash) ○

● Amathus

○ Philadelphia (Amman)

● Esbus

Callirrhoe ●

● Machaerus

Dead Sea

● Karak

NABATEANS

Gadara, Philadelphia (Amman), and Pella—had been damaged. Pompey restored these cities and granted them independence. This area of Jordan was then known as the Decapolis ("ten cities"), and the city-states agreed to pay taxes to the Romans.

Twenty years later, Rome's leader Julius Caesar (100?–44 BC) was assassinated. When the power of the Roman Empire paused, the Nabataeans saw the opportunity to extend their control. They partnered with the Parthians—warriors based in Mesopotamia and Persia—and attacked Roman strongholds. The Nabataean-Parthian partnership was not only unsuccessful but proved to be a vital mistake for the Nabataeans. Fearing the possibility of continual uprisings, the local Roman enforcer Herod the Great periodically attacked Nabataean strongholds. By the time of Pompey's death in 4 BC, Nabataean power had been reduced. By AD 106, Nabataean lands in southern Jordan were peacefully incorporated into Arabia, now a Roman province. A new capital was established at Bosra, Syria, under the Roman emperor Trajan.

As was common, Roman engineers immediately moved into Jordan to redesign its cities to reflect Roman tastes. Large forts were built near Petra and Karak along the King's Highway. By AD 114, a new road running from Bosra through Jordan to the Red Sea at Aqaba was also in place. Trajan and his descendants, Hadrian and Septimius

This stone tablet shows the edicts of Constantine the Great (275–337). At the time of its creation, between 306 and 313, it permitted Christianity as a religion of practice for all Romans. Constantine ordered property seized during earlier times of Christian persecution to be returned, provided food and protection to children, and forbade the separation of related slaves.

This Byzantine mosaic, which shows the ancient town of Memphis, is from the Church of St. John in Khirbet El-Samra, Jordan.

Severus, led Jordan through a period of cultural and economic growth. Overland trade from Arabia was flowing through Palmyra in the north, and trade along the Red Sea through Aqaba was also flourishing.

Roman control focused on Jordan's populated western regions, leaving its desert lands vulnerable. In 260, Persian forces known as Sassanians recognized this deficiency and invaded from the north. In order to preserve the strength and vastness of his empire, the Roman emperor Diocletian was forced to take action. He split the empire into eastern and western administrations, each with its own emperor. Jordan was included in the eastern portion under the leadership of Constantine (275–337), who is remembered as the emperor who embraced Christianity, the religion based on the teachings of Jesus Christ. Followers of Christianity are called Christians, and they are generally members of one of three major groups—Roman Catholic, Protestant, or Eastern Orthodox. These groups, or sects, have different beliefs about Jesus and his teachings. Under Constantine's leadership, new roadways were built in Jordan and its prosperity continued.

With his full support, Christianity began to spread throughout Constantine's empire. Much stronger than the extent of its practice, Christianity soon experienced explosive growth when Constantine converted in 324, declaring Christianity the official religion of his eastern empire. For three hundred years, the Romans and Christianity were the dominant political and religious forces in the Middle East. Known as the Byzantine period (324–636), their rule would not come to an end until the rise of Islam in the mid-seventh century.

3 ENTER THE ARABS

The Byzantine era brought steady growth, expansive construction projects, and artistic developments to Jordan. It was also during this time that Constantine's mother, Helena, started the trend of taking a pilgrimage by traveling to Jerusalem for the first time in 326. The pilgrimage routes through Jordan would later become bargaining elements in its history.

By 395, Christianity was the dominant religion in the region. Beginning then and continuing through the reign of the Byzantine emperor Justinian (527–565), both church building and the art of decorative mosaics experienced a golden age. Dual disasters, however, would bring this artistic period—and ultimately the empire—to an end.

The first of these disasters was a plague, an epidemic fatal disease, which virtually devastated the population during Justinian's rule. The second was the result of battles between Byzantine and Sassanian forces that fought violently for more than eighty years. These conflicts

This historic map of Egypt, Palestine, and Arabia was conceived by the famous seventeenth-century Dutch cartographer Willem Janszoon Blaeu (1571–1638) who was also responsible for publishing a sixty-map volume in 1630 entitled *Atlantis Appendix*. After the death of famed cartographer Abraham Ortelius, Blaeu went on to publish later editions of the world-famous *Theatrum Orbis Terrarum* (*Theatre of the World*). Blaeu later became the official cartographer for the British East India Company.

came to an end in 628, when the Sassanians recaptured Syria.

Followers of Muhammad

While Byzantine and Sassanian forces were battling in the north, an Arab holy man known as Muhammad (571–632) was gaining a significant following in the south. Muhammad's influence was growing among Jordan's desert tribes. Muhammad is considered the father of Islam; his followers are referred to as Muslims. The newly established Sassanian rule would falter after the first Muslim advances near Karak in 629, only one year after regaining control of the region; but the victory was short lived.

Muhammad died in Mecca in 632, but his armies continued to exert their power. Led by Muhammad's first caliph (successor) Abu Bakr (died 634) and driven by the zeal of a new religion, Muslim armies continued north. In 635, they seized Damascus. The following year, they defeated the entire Byzantine army on the banks of

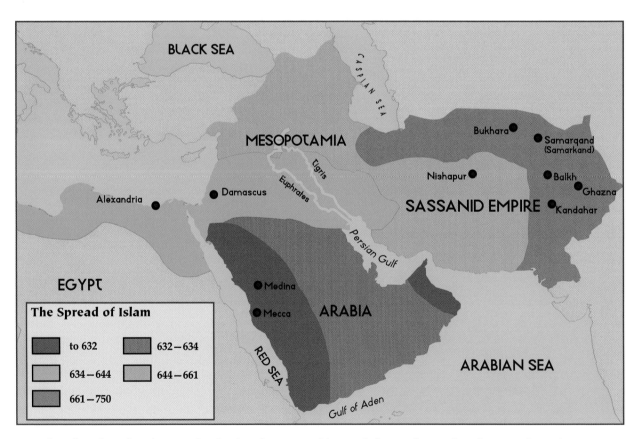

The Spread of Islam

to 632	632 – 634
634 – 644	644 – 661
661 – 750	

Within decades of Muhammad's death, Islam spread beyond the confines of Arabia, reaching the region known as the Levant, including Jordan, around AD 644. Gaining plenty of converts throughout the Middle East and Asia, by 650, the entire Persian Empire fell under the spell of Islam. The religion dominates many Middle Eastern countries to this day and is quickly becoming the world's most widely practiced faith.

Islam

Islam is the name given to the religion preached by the prophet Muhammad, beginning in approximately AD 600. Islam is now the world's second largest religion, built on three historic divisions and the central concept of *tawhid*, or the oneness of God (Allah). Any person who follows the teachings of Islam is called a Muslim.

The majority of Muslims belong to the Sunni division. Most conservative or fundamentalist Muslims are Sunnis who follow a strict approach to religion, rejecting modern and popular interpretation of Islamic law. The next largest division is the Shia, whose members are called Shiites. Among the Shiites, the Imami are the largest group. Finally, the smallest grouping of Islamic followers is the Kharijites. These Muslims believe in a precise interpretation of the Koran and are renowned for their belief in total equality under God.

the River Yarmouk between present-day Jordan and Syria.

After the Yarmouk victory, Muslim armies took less than a decade to completely dismantle Byzantine control over the Levant. Their forces were so strong that, by 656, all of Persia and the Middle East were ruled from Arabia. The next five years would be marked by Muslim turmoil.

The Koran was compiled during the caliphate of Uthman (644–658), whose reign was brought to an end by an assassin. Uthman was succeeded by the Prophet's cousin and son-in-law Ali, who was the last of the four so-called orthodox caliphs. Ali was assassinated in 661.

The Umayyad and 'Abbasid Dynasties

Muslim leadership did not stabilize until 661 when Syrian governor Muawiya I (died 680), a member of the Umayyad clan, was named caliph after Ali's murder. The Umayyads were the first great Arab dynasty whose capital was based in Damascus. Although Muawiya's appointment as caliph ended the civil war, a rift among Muslims was also created during that time.

This conflict, which persists to this day, concerns the difference in the beliefs between various Muslim sects. A division of Islam known as Sunni—the most conservative or fundamental followers of Islam—accepted Muawiya. The minority group of Muslims, the Shia, believed succession should have stayed with a relative of Muhammad. Most Muslims are Sunni, including the majority of Muslims who live in Jordan.

After several unsuccessful battles during the 630s, Arab armies united in their efforts to topple the Byzantine Empire. By 635, Arab armies had seized Damascus. A year later, similar conflicts on the banks of the Yarmouk River (on the border between present-day Syria and Jordan) allowed Arab armies to gain additional ground in the region. Soon Damascus became the capital of the successful and prosperous Umayyad Empire (661–750), shown here in this map during its height in 737. Remains of an Umayyad palace at Qasr Amra, in Jordan (inset), are but one example of Muslim architectural achievements of the period.

Although Sunni and Shia Muslims differ little in their basic beliefs, the hostility between them has led to persecution and repression of each other throughout history.

As far as Jordan was concerned, Muawiya's most significant decision was the relocation of the Muslim capital from Arabia to Jordan. In one move, Jordan found itself at the heart of the rapidly growing Umayyad Empire that extended from India to Europe.

Generous rulers, the Umayyads built lavish monuments throughout Jordan including the Dome of the Rock in Jerusalem, the Great Mosque of Damascus, and the Desert Castles, which were buildings in the country's eastern desert that served as mansions, hunting lodges, and places of negotiation. Motivated less by adherence to Islamic ideology than by the older Arab notions of honor and loyalty, Umayyad rule was tarnished by internal struggles largely based on its religious tolerance.

In 747, a massive earthquake devastated most of Jordan and severely weakened Umayyad power.

In 750, the Umayyads were overthrown by the 'Abbasids, a highly centralized Muslim monarchy. The new regime followed a stricter interpretation of Islam. The 'Abbasids relocated the Muslim capital east to Baghdad, now in Mesopotamia, instantly reducing Jordan's importance.

Although perpetually fighting the Egyptian-based Fatimid dynasty and the Seljuks from Turkey, the 'Abbasids retained control for more than two hundred years. In 969, however, the Fatimids wrestled away control of Palestine, Jordan, and southern Syria. In 1037, the Seljuks conquered the remainder of 'Abbasid territory, thereby ending their reign. By the mid-eleventh century, Seljuk Turks also controlled Jordan.

Saladin, a man of Kurdish descent, is remembered more as a diplomat than a warrior. He eventually became vizier of Egypt, overcoming Fatimid rulers in 1171. By 1187, he was responsible for regaining Jerusalem in the name of Islam.

The Crusades

The Muslim conquest sweeping the Holy Land did not go unnoticed by Western powers. In 1095, Pope Urban II launched an appeal for a unified European force to intervene in the Middle East. His goal was to restore Christian rule in Palestine and to liberate Jerusalem. These Christian holy wars are known as the Crusades.

Two years later, about one hundred thousand European troops arrived at Constantinople, which is modern-day Istanbul. In 1099, they seized Jerusalem, slaughtering everyone in the city. Within forty years, there was a strip of Christian-controlled land that ran from southern Turkey to Aqaba.

In 1144, Muslim forces in Syria started to challenge the crusaders' realm. Their success inspired a wave of Muslim resistance led by Kurdish officer Salah ad-Din al-Ayyubi, known as Saladin (1138–1193), that united the Muslim world. The Muslim goal was to oust the crusaders and retake Jerusalem, coastal Palestine, and Jordan. This goal was accomplished under Saladin in 1187.

4 MAMLUKS, TURKS, AND INDEPENDENCE

Saladin died in 1193, but his Ayyubid dynasty continued to rule the region from Cairo. The crusaders were undaunted by their defeat and continued to send forces to fight Muslim armies. Rule of the Levantine coastal areas shifted constantly. To maintain control, the Ayyubids became militarily dependent on a band of highly disciplined slave troops known as Mamluks, largely of Turkish or Mongol descent.

Mamluks

Purchased by Ayyubid military men, the Mamluk slaves were trained to fight. Their military skills grew so strong that in 1250, they were able to unite against their masters to assume control of the entire region. The Mamluk era has been called a combination of corruption and cruelty tempered with exquisite devotion to art.

The map of Palestine shown on these pages depicts the region as it was under the control of Ottoman Turks. Created between 1790 and 1800 by mapmaker Philip De Bay, it illustrates a Palestine divided into several *sanjaks*, or districts, the administration of which was largely left up to Arab Palestinians.

This Mamluk stronghold inside the eleventh-century Krak des Chevaliers (Castle of the Knights) in Syria was added after the fortress was captured by Baybars in 1271. Called the finest castle in the world by T. E. Lawrence, Krak des Chevaliers contains at least thirteen towers, several halls, bridges, passages, stables, a bakery, and a tearoom. It is actually a castle within a castle.

Less than a decade after coming to power, however, the Mamluks faced the destructive forces of a Mongol army led by Genghis Khan's grandson Hülagü (1217–1265). Their empire survived the first Mongol attack in 1258 by defeating Hülagü in Galilee, in the northernmost part of Palestine surrounded by the Mediterranean Sea, the Jordan River, and the Sea of Galilee. The victorious general Baybars (1233–1277) claimed the title of sultan and proceeded to eject the remaining crusaders out of the Levant.

During the fourteenth century, the Mamluks were able to unify Syria and Egypt, providing a period of relative peace in Jordan. Returning to its role as a point of trade along the King's Highway, Jordan survived one more Mongol push under Timur (1336–1405), also known as Tamerlane, in 1400. His advance overran most of Syria and stressed Mamluk power, which relied heavily on Red Sea trade. By the turn of the century, Jordan was poised to change hands again when Ottoman Turks from northwestern Turkey seized Constantinople, completely eliminating the Byzantine Empire.

The Ottomans

Ottoman Turks were the last major external rulers of Jordan and the Levant. Their rule began with a conquest in 1517, by Ottoman leader Selim I (1470–1520). His forces captured Lebanon, Syria, Palestine, Egypt, and Jordan, taking control of the Muslim pilgrimage route from Turkey to Arabia. Establishing a capital in Damascus, Jordan once again became part of an occupied territory.

Aside from small villages along the Muslim pilgrimage route to Mecca, the infrastructure of Jordan declined. The only regional power that remained was in the hands of

Ottoman Empire

The Ottoman Empire was the most powerful empire in the world during the 1500s and 1600s. At its height, it controlled what is now Turkey and parts of northern Africa, southwestern Asia, and southeastern Europe. The empire began around 1300 when a Turkish Muslim warrior known as Osman began to lead raids on Christian Byzantine settlements in western Anatolia—the Asian part of Turkey, located between the Black Sea and the Mediterranean Sea. Ottoman rule lasted until 1922.

The Ottomans were nomadic Turkish tribes that migrated to the Middle East from central Asia. The term "Ottoman" comes from Osman, the founder and first ruler of the empire. The Osman family ruled the Ottoman state in unbroken succession until the dynasty's twentieth-century decline. These rulers were known as sultans.

the country's eastern desert-dwelling Bedouin. As a result of the Turks' lack of governing, the Jordanian people escaped Turkish influence and remained true to their Arab identity, culture, and religion.

During the next three hundred years, Egyptian uprisings weakened the power of Ottoman rulers in Jordan. Were it not for the intervention of the British in the early 1800s, Egyptian forces appeared to be well on their way to ousting the Ottomans

altogether. Turkish forces spent a century in decline before being permanently overthrown in the early twentieth century.

At the turn of the century, Sharif Hussein of Mecca created a plan for Jordan to be part of a unified Arabian state. Hussein envisioned himself and his descendants ruling a reawakened empire, reviving it to a glory not seen since the 'Abbasid dynasty.

The Arab Revolt

At the outbreak of World War I in 1914, the Ottoman ruler Muhammad V aligned the Ottoman Empire with the Germans. This brought Turkish powers into fierce conflict with Great Britain, France, and Russia. Feeling the pressure of the Allies, Muhammad V declared a jihad, or holy war, against the West. Western forces recognized the magnitude of this action and sought out Hussein for support.

A direct descendant of the prophet Muhammad, Hussein was a very influential leader. Before taking action, he corresponded with the British high commissioner in Egypt, Sir Henry McMahon. In 1915, Hussein secured a commitment from the British to support Arab claims for independence if he incited a unified Muslim uprising against the Turks. These ten letters came to be known as the McMahon Correspondence.

This historic map of Europe, circa 1600, illustrates the Turkish Ottoman Empire at its approximate height of power. Ottoman territories were at their greatest extent after the defeat of the Mamluks and acquisition of former lands of the Persians, as well as the siege of Vienna in 1529 by Süleyman the Magnificent. The Ottoman conquest now spanned more than one million square miles and included land in sections of Europe, Arabia, and Africa, as well as all of Asia Minor, present-day Syria, Jordan, and most of Iraq.

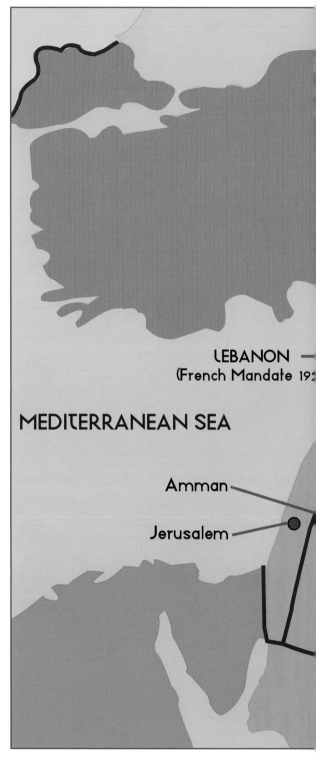

Hussein took McMahon at his word, and on June 16, 1916, he declared war on the Turks and pro-claimed Arab inde-pendence.

Hussein and two of his sons — Abdullah and Faysal — amassed nearly thirty thou-sand Arab tribesmen and seized Mecca as well as Jeddah, a major seaport of the Red Sea, from Ottoman forces. A second lieutenant in the British army, T. E. Lawrence (1888–1935), later known as Lawrence of Arabia, worked along-side Hussein and his sons against the Turks. On July 9, 1917, Lawrence and the Arab forces under his leadership staged a surprise attack and captured the all-important port city of Aqaba from the Ottomans.

Arab and British forces continued to work their way northward from Aqaba, capturing Amman in 1918. Ottoman rule in the Levant ended on October 1, 1918, with a successful assault in Damascus. With this victory, Hussein had achieved the first step in attaining Arab independence.

British Betrayals

A secret agreement known as the Sykes-Picot Agreement was signed in 1916 after the McMahon Correspondence, but before the Arab

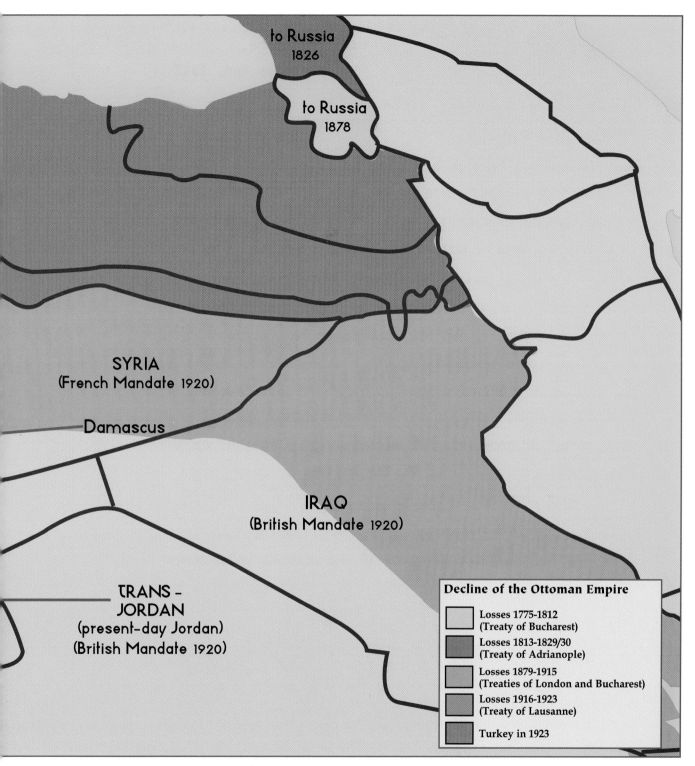

to Russia
1826

to Russia
1878

SYRIA
(French Mandate 1920)

Damascus

IRAQ
(British Mandate 1920)

TRANS-
JORDAN
(present-day Jordan)
(British Mandate 1920)

Decline of the Ottoman Empire

Losses 1775-1812
(Treaty of Bucharest)

Losses 1813-1829/30
(Treaty of Adrianople)

Losses 1879-1915
(Treaties of London and Bucharest)

Losses 1916-1923
(Treaty of Lausanne)

Turkey in 1923

Thomas Edward Lawrence *(opposite top left)*, known as Lawrence of Arabia (1888–1935), as he appeared in 1927. A well-known British archaeologist, soldier, and writer, Lawrence joined the Arab forces under Faisal I and became a military leader. Later he was an advocate for Arab independence. The map above illustrates how the Ottoman Empire declined during the eighteenth and nineteenth centuries. Territorial losses were the result of the Russo-Turkish Wars (1806–1812 and 1828-1829), World War I (1914-1918), and the 1897 Turko-Greek War. The conclusion of World War I also divided former Arab lands into mandated territories under the British and the French.

Foreign Office,

November 2nd, 1917.

Dear Lord Rothschild,

I have much pleasure in conveying to you, on behalf of His Majesty's Government, the following declaration of sympathy with Jewish Zionist aspirations which has been submitted to, and approved by, the Cabinet

"His Majesty's Government view with favour the establishment in Palestine of a national home for the Jewish people, and will use their best endeavours to facilitate the achievement of this object, it being clearly understood that nothing shall be done which may prejudice the civil and religious rights of existing non-Jewish communities in Palestine, or the rights and political status enjoyed by Jews in any other country".

I should be grateful if you would bring this declaration to the knowledge of the Zionist Federation.

[signature: Arthur James Balfour]

Shown here in its original form, this 1917 letter from Lord Arthur James Balfour to Lord Rothschild—both members of the British Parliament—later became known as the Balfour Declaration. It was the first official correspondence that recognized the importance of the creation of an independent Jewish state. It was published about a week later in the *Times* of London. Some historians surmised that one possible reason for the outspoken British conviction was an effort to drum up support for their cause in World War I.

revolt. It was a contract between the British, French, and Russian governments that divided the Middle East into permanent colonies to be ruled by Britain and France. Unknown to Hussein, the Sykes-Picot Agreement superseded any British promises regarding Arab independence. Under the agreement, France was given power in southeastern Turkey, Lebanon, Syria, and northern Iraq. Great Britain received a stretch of land from Haifa, the chief seaport in modern-day Israel, to Baghdad and the Persian Gulf area. Most of Palestine was to be administered by an international body.

The British government made another promise in 1917, to a third group, betraying Hussein and the tone of the McMahon Correspondence once again. Known as the Balfour Declaration, this letter written by British foreign secretary Arthur Balfour to the leader of Britain's Jewish community supported the creation of a "National Home for Jewish People" in Palestine. After the discovery of this document, Hussein realized the betrayal of the British government and the unlikelihood of attaining real independence for Jordan.

Establishing the Emirate

At the end of World War I, Arab forces controlled modern Saudi Arabia, Jordan, and parts of Syria. The Sykes-Picot Agreement, however, had divided the Arab lands between Britain and France. For Jordan, this marked the beginning of a thirty-year period in the country's history known as the British Mandate.

In early 1921, Jordan became a recognized state under British rule. The country's borders were formally established in 1922, and on May 15, 1923, Hussein's son Abdullah was officially named *emir*, or ruler, of the Emirate of Jordan. He established his capital in Amman where it remains today. His brother, Faysal, was named as ruler of Iraq.

5 INDEPENDENCE AND THE PALESTINIAN DILEMMA

LEBANON
French Mandate
1920–43

CYPRUS

PALESTINE
British Mandate
1920–48

EGYPT

The territory of Jordan under Abdullah Hussein's control was rugged, under-developed, and in a state of anarchy. The borders drawn by the British colonial secretary Winston Churchill were largely arbitrary, and they often dissected tribal lands. Syria, out of which Lebanon was carved, was still controlled by the French; Faysal was ruling Iraq; Jordan was under the leadership of Abdullah Hussein; and Palestine was under the thumb of the British. By 1924, an Arabian tribe led by Abd al-Aziz al-Saud further divided the Arab heartland by invading Hejaz in western Saudi Arabia, declaring it independent.

Although Arab control in the Middle East was his dream, Sharif Hussein was unable to experience it, forbidden by British forces from attaining power. Forced into exile in 1924, he left

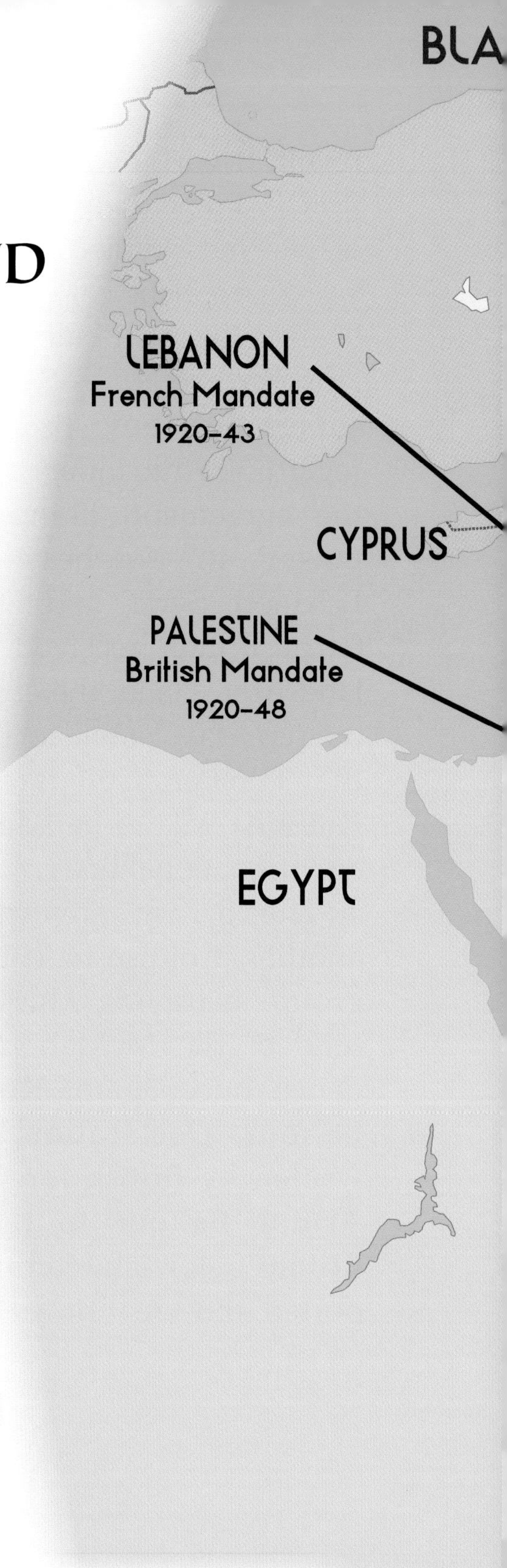

This map illustrates the divisions of Middle Eastern lands after World War I, the signing of the Sykes-Picot Agreement, the Treaty of Sévres, and the territory assignments made in 1920 under League of Nations (United Nations) mandates.

Mecca for Cyprus where he lived until his death in 1951.

Partnerships, Problems, and Palestine

Abdullah knew he needed British financial support if his country were to survive long enough to gain independence. Arab nationalists were not able to understand Abdullah's ongoing compromises with the British, however, and resentment grew. In 1928, Abdullah was able to stabilize some of the internal politicking of his country by instituting the first Jordanian constitution. Representative elections that put Jordanians in power for the first time followed one year later. Abdullah next turned his attention to the ever-intensifying situation with Palestine.

At various times throughout history, parts of modern-day Israel, Jordan, the West Bank and Gaza, and Egypt were Palestinian territories. Although Arabs have also made up the majority of Palestine's population, many Jews believe the region is theirs by divine prophecy, promised to them by God. Like most Arab countries, Palestine had only a small native Jewish community. This disparity between who rules and who is ruled set the Holy Land as a stage of conflict for many years.

Oppressed Jews from central and eastern Europe began arriving in Palestine in the early 1880s. Unified by the belief that this Holy Land was theirs by destiny, the Zionist movement was born in the nineteenth century. Zionism—from Zion, the Hebrew name for Palestine—is the term applied to the movement to establish a Jewish national state in Palestine. This eventually led to the establishment of Israel in 1948.

Zionism was founded on the prospect of making Palestine an independent Jewish nation. The 1917 Balfour Declaration, which was interpreted differently by Zionists,

Theodor Herzl (1860–1904), seen in this undated photograph, was a Hungarian liberal Jew and a Zionist leader who pushed for an independent Jewish state. He is considered the father of the Zionist Movement, after an organization that he founded in 1897.

Arabs, and the British government because of its ambiguous wordings, recognized the Zionistic claim on Palestine, supporting this notion.

Arabs, on the other hand, opposed the idea of a national Jewish state. Believing that Great Britain would simply hand Palestine to the Jews, a national Palestinian Arab movement quickly developed. On several occasions, riots and demonstrations were mounted against both British and Zionist forces. Abdullah recognized that without true independence Britain was in a position to force the Balfour Declaration into reality, bringing Arab fears to fruition. To prevent this from happening, he prepared a compromise proposition.

Abdullah proposed that if the Jews would accept the creation of a single Jordanian-Palestinian state with himself as ruler, he would support a system of Jewish self-government. This proposal, he believed, would secure the Jewish position in Palestine without displacing its existing population. It would also bring much-needed non-British money into Jordan. The Jews wanted more than political independence under a Muslim ruler, however, and rejected Abdullah's proposal.

Throughout the 1920s and 1930s, the anti-Zionist feeling among Palestinian Arabs exploded. Arabs wanted no part of Jewish immigration into Palestine and attempted to bring it to a complete halt. Hajj Amin al-Husseini, a *mufti* (spokesperson) of Jerusalem, was the Muslim hardliner who led the anti-Jewish movement. Hajj Amin was also against any peace-making agreement between Arab and Jewish leaders and used his power to cast Arab doubts on Abdullah's leadership.

Jewish immigration into Jordan, both legal and underground, intensified in 1933 with the rise of Adolf Hitler and his Nazi soldiers. Arab violence against the Jews also increased.

By 1937, war seemed close at hand. Britain's Royal Commission was concerned about its position in the Middle East and recommended partitioning Palestine between the Arabs and the Jews. They were most concerned about British access to trade routes and oil deposits recently discovered in Saudi Arabia. Palestinian leadership flatly rejected the proposal, as did the Jews. Now desperate to secure a Middle Eastern foothold, the British government, in 1939, offered full independence to the people of Palestine over a graduated ten-year period. Until the decade was over, the transfer or

Arab and Jewish recruits march side by side in this photograph taken during training exercises in Palestine, circa 1940. Officially known as Palestinians, the volunteer soldiers put aside all political and racial differences to form the Auxiliary Military Pioneer Corps for service in the British army.

purchase of land to or by the Jews, as well as Jewish immigration in general, would be subject to Arab approval. Britain's proposal was again declined.

As World War II (1939–1945) began, no decision existed regarding Palestine and thousands of Jewish immigrants. Although tensions were high, Palestinian Arabs and Jews entered World War II fighting side-by-side with the British and Allied powers against the Axis powers of Germany, Italy, and Japan.

During World War II, Jordan was exempt from suffering. Upon the liberation of Europe, however, Zionist forces in Palestine pressured the British to permit the immigration of several hundred thousand Jewish survivors of the Holocaust. The tensions caused by this arrival of immigrants cast a foreboding shadow on Jordan's future.

6 THE RISE OF THE HASHEMITE KINGDOM

The British Mandate over Jordan ended in 1946, permanently securing its independence. In May of the following year, the title emir was changed to king, a position claimed by Abdullah.

At about this same time, a United Nations Special Commission on Palestine recommended that the territory be divided into an Arab and a Jewish state, with Jerusalem—the most disputed of all Palestinian territories—under international control. The UN General Assembly adopted this plan on November 29, 1947. Jews had attained their goal of a recognized Jewish state, however, they were unhappy about being denied Jerusalem. Arabs were also upset by the UN's actions, since they were opposed to the creation of any kind of Jewish state in Palestine. Fighting broke out immediately.

The First Arab-Israeli War

In May 1948, upon the withdrawal of British troops and the expiration of the British Mandate, the Jews proclaimed an independent nation of Israel. On May 15, 1948, only one day after the British troops withdrew from Palestine and Israel's declaration of independence, fighting began. The Jordanian army, known then as the Arab Legion, joined forces with

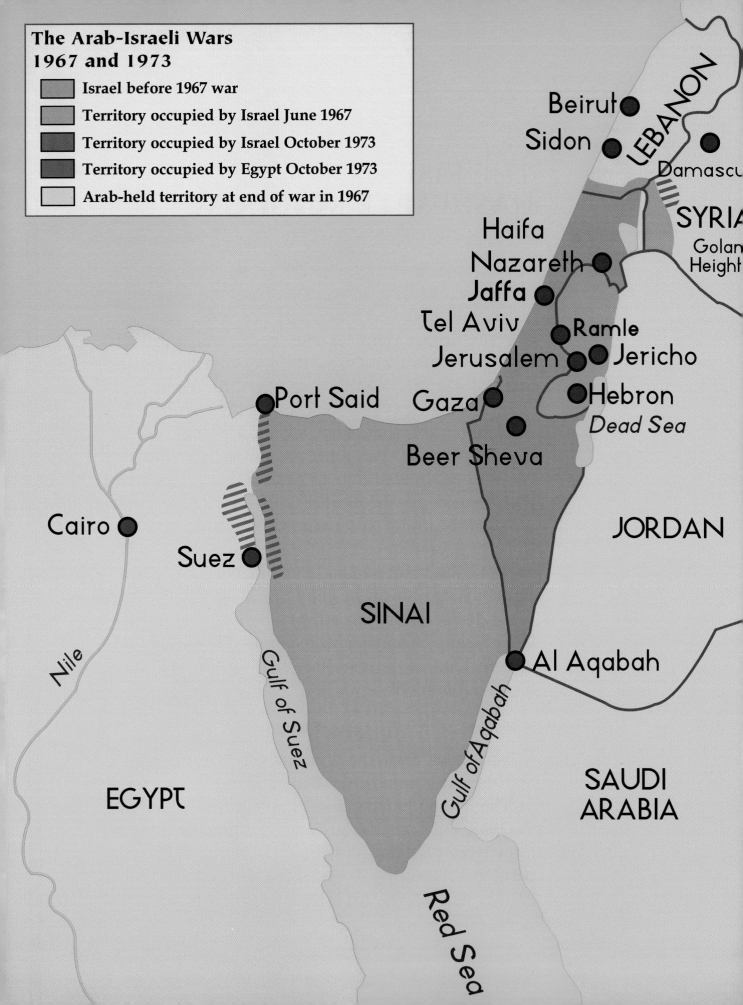

The Arab-Israeli Wars 1967 and 1973

- Israel before 1967 war
- Territory occupied by Israel June 1967
- Territory occupied by Israel October 1973
- Territory occupied by Egypt October 1973
- Arab-held territory at end of war in 1967

Beirut

Sidon

LEBANON

Damascus

SYRIA

Golan Heights

Haifa

Nazareth

Jaffa

Tel Aviv

Ramle

Jerusalem

Jericho

Gaza

Hebron

Port Said

Dead Sea

Beer Sheva

JORDAN

Cairo

Suez

SINAI

Al Aqabah

Nile

Gulf of Suez

Gulf of Aqabah

EGYPT

SAUDI ARABIA

Red Sea

Israeli Arabs and the nations of the Arab League to attack Israel. In 1948, the Arab League consisted of seven Arab countries (Iraq, Saudi Arabia, the Lebanese Republic, Yemen, Jordan, Egypt, and Syria) and was created for the purpose of coordinating international Arab policy and limiting aspirations for a Jewish nation in Palestine. The combined Arab armies fought Jewish forces in what became known as the first Arab-Israeli War.

When the fighting ended a year later, Jordan held the West Bank and the eastern portion of Jerusalem, which included many of the city's holiest places. Israel mostly occupied Palestine, including the Galilee region in the northeast, as well as the cities of Haifa, Jaffa, Lydda, and Ramle. Egypt held the Israel-bordered Gaza Strip.

In April 1949, Abdullah officially changed the name of his country to the Hashemite Kingdom of Jordan. Hashemite refers to Hashim, the great-grandfather of the prophet Muhammad, from whom the Jordanian royal house claims direct descent. He also signed an armistice with Israel establishing a boundary to the Jordan-controlled West Bank known as the Green Line.

Hundreds of thousands of Palestinian Arabs fled or were forced from their homes in territories that were now part of the newly established Israel. Most sought refuge in the West Bank. After the war, Jordan's population soared from 435,000 to 1.5 million.

In 1950, despite opposition from the Arab League, Abdullah formally merged all of Arab-held Palestine with Jordan and granted Jordanian citizenship to West Bank residents. Jordan governed the West Bank for the next seventeen years, although relations between Jordanian nationals and West Bank Palestinians remained strained.

King Hussein

On July 20, 1951, a Palestinian national opposed to Jordan's tolerance of Israel assassinated Abdullah in Jerusalem. Abdullah was briefly succeeded by his son Talal I, who was deposed only one month after assuming the throne because of a mental disorder. Talal's teenage

Tensions were so great between Jordan and other Arab nations that, by the mid-1960s, King Hussein declared martial law in the country. This map shows territories gained by Israel in the Six-Day War in 1967 and the Arab-Israeli War of 1973. The Israeli occupation of these territories increased the rate of Palestinian refugees who immigrated into Jordan, pushing the country further into an economic crisis. Jordanian armies participated in the Arab-Israeli War of 1948-1949 as well as the Six-Day War, which caused the country massive human and territorial losses. By June 11, 1967, Jordan lost half of its territory, a third of its population, much-needed agricultural land, and both Muslim and Christian holy sites in Jerusalem.

son, Hussein I, became king the same day.

The early years of King Hussein's reign were fraught with unrest throughout the country. The dramatic increase in Jordan's Palestinian population caused political riots and economic divisions. Jordan's lack of food, shelter, and basic services was now widespread.

Jordan began to develop petroleum refining, cement and phosphate industries, as well as agriculture, manufacturing, and tourism-based economies. Politically, however, the country was in a state of turmoil as Palestinians competed for power with East Bank Jordanians who controlled the government. On the international front, Arab countries continued competing for dominance in the Middle East. The United States and the Soviet Union also sought to extend influence in the region.

International Acceptance

During the 1950s, Jordan remained unstable despite becoming a member of the United Nations in 1955. Less than one year later, Jordanian and UN delegates fought over border violations and armed raids. In 1957, there was even an attempt to overthrow the Hussein government.

A bright spot appeared for Jordan shortly after the attempted coup, however, when on January 17, 1957, a ten-year pact was signed by Egypt, Syria, and Saudi Arabia. The treaty provided an annual subsidy of $36 million dollars for Jordan to reduce its reliance on Western powers—specifically Great Britain—and sever ties that these countries considered to be anti-Arab and pro-Israel.

Only three months later, Egypt and Syria revoked the aid pact. By the end of the year, they had formed the United Arab Republic (UAR). In response, King Hussein allied with his Hashemite cousins in Iraq to create the Arab Federation. Both alliances were temporary, however, and by the end of the 1950s, the United States became Jordan's chief Western source of support.

Arab-Israeli Conflict

The fight between Arabs and Jews in the Middle East over Palestine is referred to as the Arab-Israeli conflict. This conflict has led to several wars

King Hussein I, pictured here in a military uniform, is remembered for being one of the greatest leaders and diplomats of the twentieth century. Throughout his forty-seven-year reign, he led Jordan soon after the time of its independence, through its rise as a nation, to its conflicts with neighboring Arab countries. Through it all he pushed for the continual peace process in the Middle East, including talks with former U.S. president Bill Clinton in 1998, when he said, "We [Arab nations] have no right to dicate, through irresponsible action or narrow-mindedness, the future of our children and our children's children. There has been enough destruction, enough death, and enough waste."

Israeli soldiers stand triumphant in this photograph following their recapture of the United Nations Headquarters from Jordanian forces in Jerusalem at the end of the Six-Day War. This photograph was taken on June 8, 1967.

among Arab nations, Palestinian refugees, and Israel. The Arab-Israeli War of 1948–1949 included the armies of Egypt, Jordan, Syria, Lebanon, and Iraq, as well as Palestinian guerrillas. In 1967, Egypt, Syria, and Jordan massed their armies on Israel's borders for the Six-Day War. Also known as the October or Ramadan War, the Arab-Israeli War of 1973 had Israel fighting the armies of Syria and Egypt.

Several peace treaties addressing the conflict have since been signed — beginning in 1979 with the Camp David Accords — but a real resolution seems unlikely.

7 WAR AND DIPLOMACY

For King Hussein and his government, the early 1960s were relatively free of internal political strife. Jordan's economy was expanding because of its potassium and phosphate industries, as well as the rise in tourism in Jordanian territories. Overall, King Hussein was building renewed infrastructure in Jordan. These improvements turned his population's attention away from differences and toward the common quest for prosperity and independence from Western monies.

Foreign relations were less relaxed, however. In 1961, Syria seceded from the United Arab Republic. Hussein recognized the new regime; and in retaliation, Egypt's President Nasser broke relations with Jordan. By the mid-1960s, even relations with Syria became strained when it allied itself with Egypt and Iraq. This loose union unleashed massive demonstrations in Jordan, a turmoil that became so great that King Hussein declared martial law.

The Palestine Liberation Organization

During the 1950s, while King Hussein was struggling to unify his country, a group of young Palestinian students was creating an organization focused on obtaining power for Palestine. The Palestine Liberation

Organization (PLO) was formed in Jerusalem in May 1964, with Yasser Arafat as its leader.

The PLO is the political body that represents the Arab people of Palestine. Its goal was to establish an independent state in Palestine, the homeland of the Arab Palestinian people. The PLO had five main goals, although all were related to one: the liberation of Palestine. To do so, the PLO required arms, self-organization, cooperation with friendly Arab forces, and cooperation with sympathetic international forces.

Arafat's PLO established its headquarters in Amman. It used Jordan as a base for vicious guerrilla attacks on Israel. In response to the PLO attacks, the Israelis retaliated against Jordanian villages. The destruction that followed resulted in an immense divide between the Jordanian government and the PLO. In 1966, Jordan formally suspended support

An Israeli soldier marches a Jordanian soldier through the streets of Bethlehem. The captive was found without identification papers after Israeli soldiers took the city in the Six-Day War in June 1967. Jordan lost control of the West Bank and East Jerusalem before a United Nations–declared cease-fire took place, ending the fighting.

for the PLO, claiming it maintained pro-Communist activities.

Jordanian relations with Syria were also suffering. Both the Syrian government and the PLO were encouraging Jordanian citizens to revolt against King Hussein, and border fighting became common along the boundaries between Jordan and Syria and Jordan, the West Bank, and Israel.

The Six-Day War

King Hussein recognized that war with Israel was inevitable. Despite the calls for Arab unity, nations tended to break apart. Extremist countries—Syria, Egypt, and Iraq— were vehemently opposed to any independence for Palestine. Moderate states—Jordan, Saudi Arabia, and Tunisia—were focused on creating a peaceful solution. Fearing that

isolation from his Arab neighbors would result in total Jordanian defeat, King Hussein flew to Cairo in 1967 to meet with Egypt's President Nasser. The result was a defense treaty that represented an unprecedented gesture of Arab solidarity.

On June 5, 1967, Israeli forces attacked. A UN cease-fire was accepted by both sides six days later, but Arab losses were intense. Israel took control of the Golan Heights (from Syria) and the Sinai Peninsula and the Gaza Strip (from Egypt). Jordan's losses were devastating. By June 11, 1967, Israel had assumed control of East Jerusalem and the entire West Bank. In less than a week, Jordan lost half of its inhabited and inhabitable territory, a third of its population, prime agricultural land, and both Muslim and Christian holy sites in Jerusalem. In one event,

West Bank

The West Bank is a territory in the Middle East that lies between Israel and Jordan. It covers about 2,270 square miles (5,880 square kilometers) and has a population of more than 2 million people, most of whom are Palestinian Arabs.

Historically part of the region known as Palestine, the West Bank was annexed by Jordan in 1950. In 1967, Israel defeated Jordan, Egypt, and Syria in the Six-Day War and took control of the West Bank. In 1993, a peace process began between Israeli and Palestinian leaders; and the next year, Israel began withdrawing from the West Bank. The two sides never reached a final agreement; and in 2002, Israel reoccupied many West Bank areas from which it had previously withdrawn.

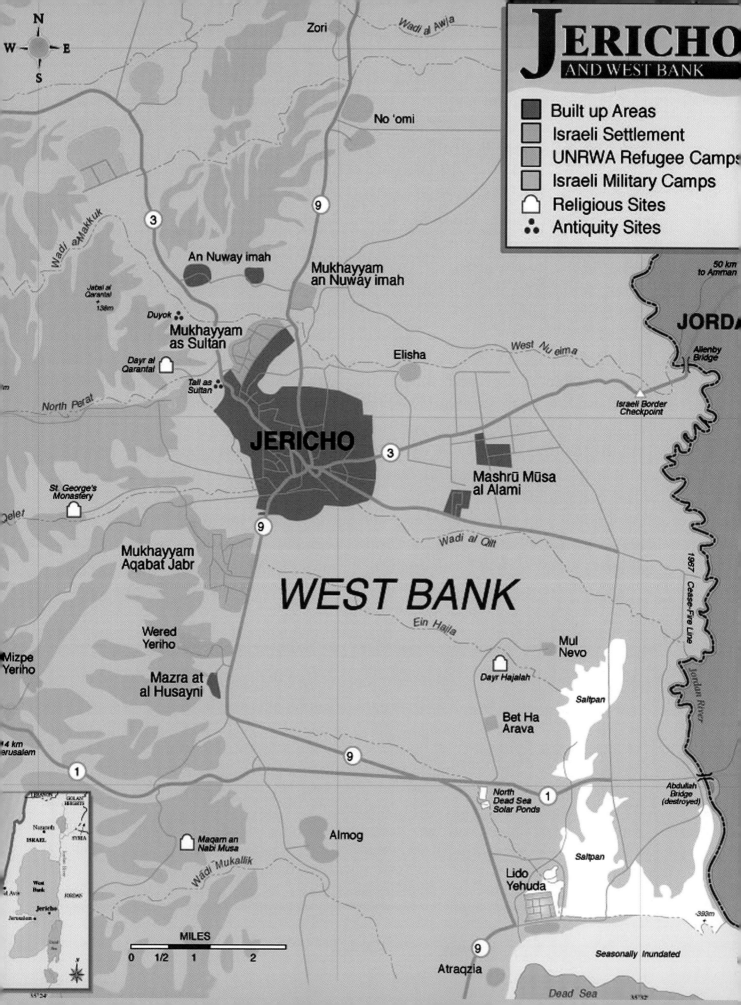

Jordan's two principal sources of income (agriculture and tourism) were gone. This war also resulted in Palestinian refugees. Nearly a quarter million Palestinians immigrated to Jordan's East Bank, stressing the government and economy once again.

After this defeat, Jordan became increasingly unsettled. Palestinians were even more militant in their anti-Israeli beliefs and more certain that King Hussein and other Arab leaders were unwilling to aid in the liberation of their homeland. Although the PLO and its guerrilla factions laid low for some time, tensions erupted again in September 1970.

Black September

In the late 1960s, the PLO and its guerrillas received money and arms from the oil-rich Gulf states (Iran, Iraq, Kuwait, Saudi Arabia, Bahrain, Qatar, the United Arab Emirates, and Oman). These resources enabled Palestinian forces to control Jordan's refugee camps, as well as to exert influence on Jordan's Palestinian population.

Support for Palestinian nationalism within Jordan resulted in the development of a *fedayeen* (martyrs) movement. The fedayeen began systematic attacks on Israel from Jordanian territory. Israeli reprisals devastated Jordan's only remaining agricultural territories in the East Bank and were undermining its government's prospects for peace between these neighboring countries. King Hussein no longer had a choice.

On September 17, 1970, the Jordanian army attacked Palestinian guerrillas in Amman, the setting of a bloody civil war. In an attempt to embarrass King Hussein, the fedayeen hijacked three commercial jetliners and flew them to northern Jordan, holding passengers and crew hostage.

Arafat and Hussein agreed to suspend fighting in October 1970, but sporadic outbursts continued. It was not until July 1971 that Jordanian forces successfully forced out the PLO. This period in Jordan's history came to be known as Black September.

Reconciliation and Recovery

King Hussein's government was back in control, but his credibility among Arab nations was severely questioned. Internally, Jordan was socially divided, with Jordanian nationals and Palestinians full of suspicion and resentment.

This map of Jericho and the West Bank shows Israeli-occupied territories after the Six-Day War in 1967. Settlements, military camps, United Nations–controlled refugee camps, and religious sites are also indicated. Jordan relinquished its control over the West Bank in 1988, and in 2002, Israel reoccupied some areas there, where its forces had previously withdrawn.

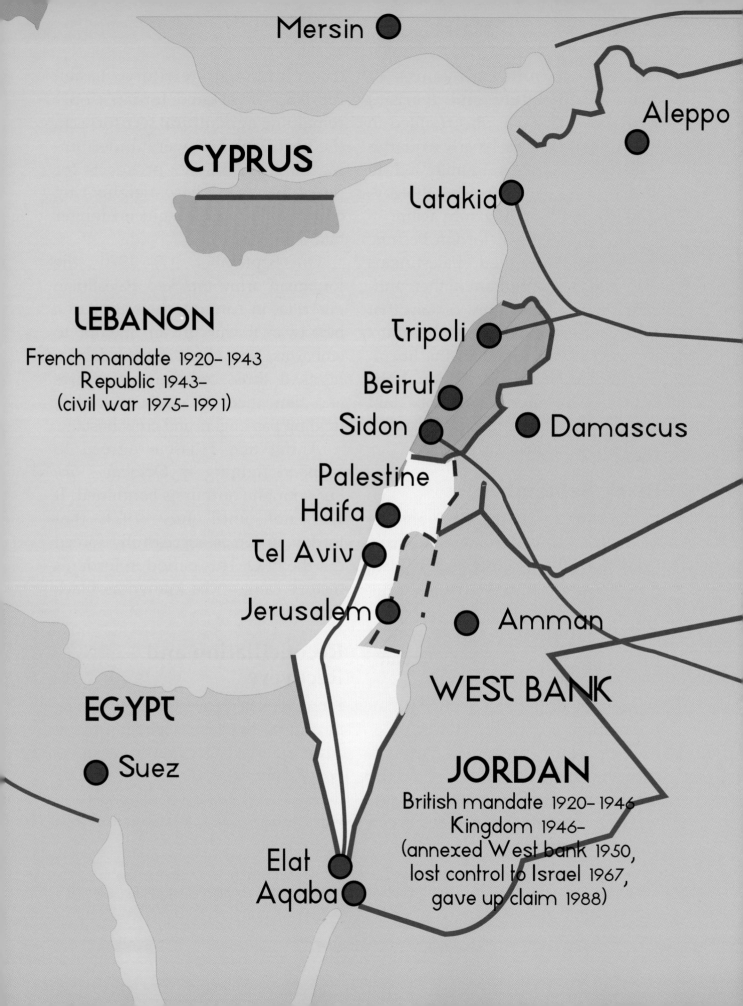

Mersin

CYPRUS

Aleppo

Latakia

LEBANON

French mandate 1920–1943
Republic 1943–
(civil war 1975–1991)

Tripoli

Beirut

Sidon

Damascus

Palestine

Haifa

Tel Aviv

Jerusalem

Amman

WEST BANK

EGYPT

JORDAN

British mandate 1920–1946
Kingdom 1946–
(annexed West bank 1950,
lost control to Israel 1967,
gave up claim 1988)

Suez

Elat

Aqaba

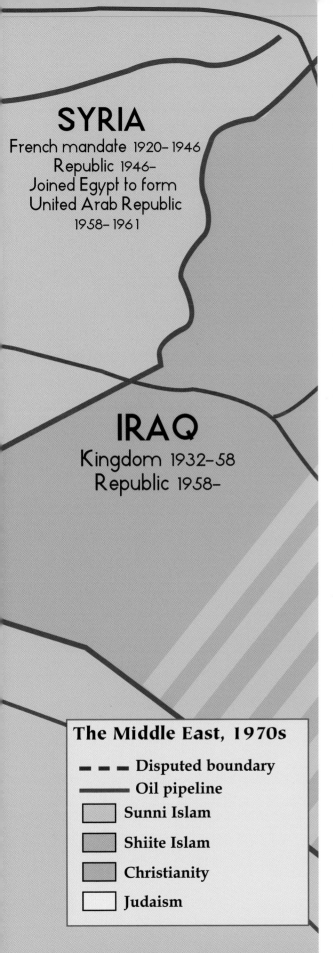

SYRIA
French mandate 1920–1946
Republic 1946–
Joined Egypt to form
United Arab Republic
1958–1961

IRAQ
Kingdom 1932–58
Republic 1958–

The Middle East, 1970s

- - - Disputed boundary
——— Oil pipeline
☐ Sunni Islam
▨ Shiite Islam
▨ Christianity
☐ Judaism

In 1972, King Hussein again proposed plans for a united Arab kingdom of Jordan and Palestine that offered virtual independence under his leadership, another idea that was openly criticized. He was now even further isolated from the rest of the Arab world.

In 1973, Jordan attended a reconciliation summit with Egypt's president Anwar Sadat and Hafez al-Assad of Syria. The result was an agreement of amnesty for all political prisoners, including PLO guerrillas. Later that year, Jordan refrained from participation in the Egyptian-Syrian October War against Israel, another decision that did not bode well for the nation.

With the power and prestige of the PLO growing by the mid-1970s, Hussein and nineteen other Arab leaders attended the Arab Summit Conference in Rabat, Morocco. The most significant outcome of the conference was the collective recognition of the PLO as the "sole legitimate representative of the Palestinian people," and the confirmation of its right to establish authority over any liberated Palestinian lands.

As the 1970s drew to a close, Jordan had relinquished its rights to the West Bank, although it still played a role in its administration. Despite the large geographic losses of the 1960s and 1970s, Jordan found itself on relatively stable ground beginning in the 1980s.

A variety of religious groups are represented across the Middle East, as seen on this map. Certainly a region known for its rapidly changing borders and frequent military upsets, the Arab countries of the Middle East are largely inhabited by a Sunni Muslim majority, though Iraqis are mostly Shiite Muslims. A small section of Syria, though not shown on this map, is inhabited by a Christian Druze population.

8 A FUTURE OF CONFLICT

WEST BANK AND
GAZA STRIP
*territories
under provisional status
since 1993*

WEST
BANK

JERUSALEM ■

Gaza ●

When Iraq invaded Iran and launched the Iran-Iraq War (1980–1988), Jordan benefited financially from the passage of goods through the seaport of Aqaba bound for Iraq. Unfortunately for Jordan, siding with Iraq in this conflict again strained relations with Syria.

The First Intifada

In the early 1980s, after a decade of Israeli-Palestinian conflicts over land and water rights throughout the West Bank and the Gaza Strip, Palestinian resistance efforts became aggressive. Under the direction of the PLO, rioting developed into the first *intifada*, the Arabic word for "uprising." Beginning in the Gaza Strip in 1987, rebellions were soon under way in the West Bank.

In 1988, after seven months of fighting, Jordan ceded to the PLO all territorial claims and financial

ISRAEL

EGYPT

This modern political map of Jordan shows the country as it currently appears. Jordan's future depends largely on its domestic agenda, controlling its rising tide of Islamists, maintaining diplomatic relationships with other Middle Eastern countries, and continuing its efforts to contribute to the region's struggle for a peaceful future.

and administrative responsibilities related to the Israeli-occupied West Bank. Israel immediately moved in and began restricting the activities of Palestinian-administered institutions. Afterward, the PLO proclaimed an independent state of Palestine. Jordan and sixty other countries recognized the new state and, in turn, supported the right of Israel to exist.

Seeming to have learned from choosing sides in the Iran-Iraq conflict years earlier, King Hussein attempted to act as a mediator after Iraq invaded Kuwait in 1990. Although he successfully straddled the political fence, Jordan's infrastructure was suffering.

The Gulf War (1990–1991)

Dependent on Iraq for nearly 25 percent of its trade and oil imports, Jordan was trapped when Iraqi president Saddam Hussein invaded Kuwait in August 1990. Jordanian public opinion backed Saddam Hussein, while in the streets of Amman, large demonstrations backing Kuwait were intense. In the end, King Hussein remained neutral, favoring a peaceful resolution.

King Hussein pleaded with the Arab League to mediate the crisis, but Saudi Arabia, Egypt, and Syria all supported Western intervention. He initiated his own peace initiatives, even addressing the U.S. Congress in 1990, urging a withdrawal of the international peacekeeping force in Saudi Arabia. When that failed, he warned of the disastrous environmental effects a war could cause. In a final plea, he aligned the Iraq-Kuwait dispute with the Arab-Israeli conflict and instigated a dialogue among all Arab leaders. His arguments went unanswered and the Persian Gulf War raged from August 1990 to March 1991.

Among Arab countries, King Hussein was highly regarded for the open declaration of his views against the war. Western powers did not feel the same, however, and after hostilities ceased in March 1991, the United States canceled Jordanian aid programs as punishment for King Hussein's neutrality. At the same time, Kuwait and other gulf states regarded their Jordanian and Palestinian population as collaborators with Iraq and expelled nearly three hundred thousand people for return to Jordan. The combination of declining financial support from the United States, the shutoff of Iraqi oil, and this latest surge of refugees was disastrous for Jordan.

Peace and Crisis

In 1991, a Jordanian national charter lifted a ban on political parties that had been in effect since 1967. Jordan's

The Persian Gulf War map showing the region during the Persian Gulf War of 1990–1991, including Turkey, Syria, Iraq, Iran, Kuwait, and Saudi Arabia.

The Persian Gulf War 1990–1991

- Southern limit of Iraqi no-fly zone in the north from 1991
- Northern limit of Iraqi no-fly zone in the south from 1992
- Oil field
- Iraqi invasion of Kuwait, August 1990
- Allied ground forces counter-attack, February 1991

TURKEY

SYRIA

IRAN

Tigris

Euphrates

⊙ Baghdad

IRAQ

⊙ Isfahan

Basra ⊙

KUWAIT ● Kuwait

Persian Gulf

SAUDI ARABIA

This map shows activity in the Persian Gulf region during the Persian Gulf War of 1990–1991. Jordan, who has maintained a peaceful relationship with Iraq, did not question Iraq's invasion of Kuwait, but tried to sustain diplomatic relations with Iraqis and Kuwaitis as well as with the United States. The no-fly zones seen in Iraq were put in place as part of U.N. Security Council Resolution 668 in the early 1990s, as a means to protect Kurds and Shia Muslims from Saddam Hussein.

first democratic elections were held in 1993. Although the majority of candidates were independents loyally supporting the king, a political group known as the Islamic Action Front gained strong support. The Islamic Action Front is the political arm of the Muslim Brotherhood, one of the most influential political and religious movements in the Middle East. The brotherhood calls for Muslim nations to establish governments based on Islamic principles, rejecting Western secular (nonreligious) ideas.

In 1994, dramatic steps toward peace in the Middle East were taken when, on October 24, King Hussein and the Israeli prime minister Yitzhak Rabin signed a peace treaty. The chief points in the peace negotiations were boundary demarcations and control of water resources, as well as the pledge to cooperate in combating terrorism. Soon, Israelis were visiting Petra, the well-preserved old city of the Nabateans, as hope for peace remained high.

A New King

Throughout the 1990s, concerns had been voiced about the health of King Hussein. In 1992, while undergoing cancer surgery, he had one of his kidneys removed. Four years later, he underwent surgery for an enlarged prostate, and in 1998, he began chemotherapy for lymph cancer. Physicians in the United States provided King Hussein's medical care.

During each of his visits to the United States, he appointed his brother Hassan as regent. Hassan was next in line for the Jordanian throne. In 1999, however, King Hussein abruptly removed Hassan from the succession and declared his son, Abdullah II, to be the crown prince.

Hussein I, king of Jordan, died on February 7, 1999, after forty-seven years in power, one of the longest reigns in history. More than fifty world leaders attended his funeral. In July 1999, his son was formally crowned King Abdullah II.

In the years since Abdullah II came to power, Jordan has remained relatively quiet in regional and world affairs. The young king has chosen instead to focus on domestic policies. Along with two other young Arab leaders—Mohammed VI of Morocco and Bashar al-Assad of Syria—today's Arab leaders are looked on as progressive rulers committed to peace, economic liberalization, and socially progressive politics.

With the ongoing struggles in the Middle East, Abdullah II will be forced to reassert Jordan as a regional power. For now, however, his focus is to rescue his country from economic depression.

Jordan's King Abdullah II applauds his wife, Queen Rania, during a ceremony marking their accession in Amman, on June 9, 1999. Thousands of Jordanians took to the streets to celebrate the accession of the king to the throne he inherited from his father, the late King Hussein, just four months before.

The Future

The September 11, 2001, attacks on New York and Washington, D.C., in the United States reinforced the desperate need for peace in the Middle East. On the whole, Jordan is considered to be far ahead of other Middle Eastern countries in terms of its efforts to continue diplomatic relationships with foreign nations. Jordanian citizens also seem supportive of their country's warm relations with the West.

As the U.S-led occupation of Iraq continued, King Abdullah II met with U.S. secretary of state Colin Powell in May 2003 to talk about the future of peace in the Middle East. At the talks, the king stressed the importance of reestablishing stability in Iraq and the necessity of forming a national government in the occupied country.

The principal challenge for King Abdullah II, in the wake of recent conflicts in the Middle East, is to preserve security and stability in Jordan. This means creating a balance in the government that incorporates democracy, tribalism, Islam, and civility among differing factions.

As a young country, Jordan needs to maintain the support of both its Middle Eastern and Western allies that will be crucial to its ultimate prosperity.

TIMELINE

9000 BC First inhabitants settle on the West Bank of the River Jordan near Jericho.

960–922 BC The reign of Solomon; upon his death, his kingdom is split into Israel in the north and Judah in the south.

597–587 BC Jerusalem, Palestine, and Jordan fall to Babylonian king Nebuchadnezzar.

538 BC The Nabateans, a desert Arab group, incorporate Jordan into their kingdom.

323 BC Alexander the Great dies, and the western part of Jordan becomes part of the Seleucid Empire.

AD 106 Under Roman emperor Trajan, Jordan becomes a province of Arabia.

661 Jordan falls under the control of the Umayyad dynasty.

1086 The Seljuk Turks invade the Middle East.

1099 Crusaders establish a kingdom in Jerusalem.

1517–1920 Ottoman Turks take control of the Middle East.

1916 Sharif Hussein proclaims the Arab revolt against the Turks in Mecca.

1917 Arab forces led by British officer T. E. Lawrence (Lawrence of Arabia) and Hussein's son capture the port of Aqaba, a key victory in the revolt against the Turks.

1920 Jordan emerges as a separate territory after the breakup of the Ottoman Empire and the execution of the secret Sykes-Picot Agreement.

1946 Jordan receives full independence.

1947 Jordan officially changes its name to the Hashemite Kingdom of Jordan.

1948 Jordan joins the Arab states in invading the newly established state of Israel. Jordan gains control of East Jerusalem and the West Bank.

1950 King Abdullah annexes the Gaza Strip, West Bank, and East Jerusalem, offering all Palestinians in these territories full Jordanian citizenship.

1951 Hussein I becomes king.

1955 Jordan becomes a member of the United Nations.

1967 The Six-Day War with Israel results in the loss of East Jerusalem and the West Bank.

1974 Hussein recognizes the PLO as the representative of the Palestinian people.

1980–1988 Jordan backs Iraq in the Iran-Iraq War.

1988 Jordan renounces the West Bank, easing relations with Israel and the PLO.

1991 Jordan declines to join the coalition against Iraq during the Persian Gulf War.

1994 Jordan signs a full peace treaty with Israel.

1999 King Hussein dies of cancer and is replaced by his son, Crown Prince Abdullah.

2000 The United States and Jordan sign the U.S.-Jordan Free Trade Agreement.

2001 Abdullah II meets with President George W. Bush to revive peace process.

2002 U.S. diplomat Laurence Foley is assassinated at his home in Amman.

2003 Abdullah II speaks with U.S. secretary of state Colin Powell about President George W. Bush's three-year "road map to peace" plan and the establishment of an independent Palestinian state.

Arab League An informal name of the League of Arab States, a voluntary association of independent countries. Its purposes are to strengthen ties among the member states, coordinate their policies, and promote their common interests.

Bedouin Wandering Arabs who live in the deserts of the Middle East.

caliph A title taken by Muslim rulers that asserts religious authority to rule derived from that of Muhammad.

caliphate The territory over which a caliph's rule extends or the time for which it lasts.

coup (coup d'etat) French term meaning "blow to the state" referring to a sudden, unexpected overthrow of a government by outsiders.

exodus The departure of the Israelites from Egypt under Moses.

Gaza Strip The region in southwestern Asia bordered on the south by Egypt, on the west by the Mediterranean Sea, and on the north and east by Israel.

guerrillas The members of a band of fighters who harass the enemy by sudden raids and ambushes.

Hashemite A member of an ancient Arab dynasty that included Muhammad.

Jerusalem The historic city lying at the intersection of Israel and the West Bank; claimed by Israel as its capital.

Mamluks Slaves converted to Islam who advanced themselves to high military posts in Egypt.

martial law Governed by a country's own army or a foreign army that has taken control.

Nabateans The ancient people of northwest Arabia.

Palestine Historic region situated on the eastern coast of the Mediterranean Sea in southwestern Asia. Palestine is now largely divided between Israel and the Israeli-occupied territories.

regent A person who rules a country when the rightful ruler cannot, either because he or she is too young, out of the country, or ill.

sharif A descendant of the prophet Muhammad through his daughter, Fatima; an Arab prince or ruler.

Sharif Hussein Arabian political and religious leader who led a revolt against the Ottoman Empire and proclaimed himself king.

Shia A sect of Islam that supports the claims of Ali and his line and their presumptive right to the caliphate and leadership of the Muslim community.

Sunni A sect of Islam that supports the traditional method of election to the caliphate and accepts the Umayyad line of rulers.

Umayyad dynasty The Islamic rulers of the Middle East from AD 661–750.

wadi A canyon in the desert where rainfall runs off the hills and soaks into the ground; these areas can be cultivated.

West Bank A territory in southwestern Asia, bounded on the north, west, and south by Israel and on the east by Jordan.

FOR MORE INFORMATION

Embassy of the Hashemite Kingdom of
    Jordan
3504 International Drive NW
Washington, DC 20008
(202) 966–2664
Web site:
    http://www.jordanembassyus.org

The Middle East Institute
1761 N Street NW
Washington, DC 20036
(202) 785-1141
Web site: http://www.mideasti.org/

Web sites

Due to the changing nature of Internet
links, the Rosen Publishing Group, Inc.,
has developed an online list of Web
sites related to the subject of this book.
This site is updated regularly. Please
use this link to access the list:

http://www.rosenlinks.com/liha/jord

FOR FURTHER READING

Foster, Leila Merrel. *Enchantment of the
    World: Jordan*. Chicago: Children's
    Press, 1999.
South, Coleman. *Jordan*. New York:
    Marshall Cavendish
    Corporation, 1997.

Stefoff, Rebecca. *Major World Nations:
    West Bank/Gaza Strip*. Philadelphia:
    Chelsea House Publishers, 1999.
Whitehead, Susan. *Major World Nations:
    Jordan*. Philadelphia: Chelsea House
    Publishers, 1999.

BIBLIOGRAPHY

Embassy of Jordan—Jordan Information
    Bureau. "History of Jordan."
    Retrieved May 13, 2002
    (http://www.embassyus.org/new/
    jib/aboutjordan/history.html).
"Jordan." CIA—The World Fact Book.
    Retrieved May 13, 2002
    (http://www.odci.gov/cia/
    publications/factbook/geos/jo.html).
"Jordan, Hashemite Kingdom of."
    Microsoft® Encarta® Online
    Encyclopedia 2002. Retrieved June
    15, 2002 (http://encarta.msn.com).
"Jordan." Infoplease.com. Retrieved
    May 23, 2002 (http://www.
    infoplease.com/ce6/wpr;d/
    A0826603.html).

Kennedy, David L. "Ancient Jordan
    From the Air." *Aramco World*,
    May/June 2000, pp. 36–46.
Metz, Helen Chapman, ed. *Jordan: A
    Country Study*. Washington, DC:
    Federal Research Division, Library
    of Congress, 1991.
Patai, Raphael. *The Kingdom of Jordan*.
    Princeton, NJ: Princeton University
    Press, 1958.
Stannard, Dorothy, Michael Ellis, and
    Brian Bell, eds. *Insight Guide Jordan*.
    New York: Langenscheidt
    Publishers, Inc., 1999.

INDEX

A

'Abbasids, 25, 26, 29
Abdullah II (son of Hussein I), 58, 59
Alexander the Great, 15
Amman (Ammon), 8, 15, 18, 32, 35, 48, 51, 56
  establishment of, 12
Arab-Israeli
  conflict, 45–46, 56
  War, 43, 46
Arab League, 43, 56
Arab Legion (Jordanian army), 41–43
Arabs
  Israeli, 43
  Muslim, 38, 49
  Palestinian, 39, 40, 43, 48, 51, 53
  revolts, 29–32, 35, 39, 41
Arab Summit Conference, 53
Arafat, Yasser, 48, 51
Ayyubid dynasty, 26

B

Balfour Declaration, 35, 38–39
Bedouins, 6, 7, 29
Black September, 51
British Mandate, 35, 41
Bronze Age, 8–11
Byzantine Empire, 19, 20–23, 28

C

Christianity, 6, 9, 19, 20, 25, 49
Constantine, 19, 20
Crusades, 25, 26, 28

E

Egypt, 5, 6, 9, 10, 11, 15, 25, 28, 29, 38, 43, 45, 46, 47, 53, 56

G

Gaza Strip, 49, 54

H

Hussein I (son of Talal), 43–45, 47, 49, 51–53, 56, 58

Hussein, Abdullah (son of Sharif), 32, 35, 36, 38, 39, 41, 43
Hussein, Faysal (son of Sharif), 32, 35, 36
Hussein, Saddam, 56, 59
Hussein, Sharif, 29–32, 35, 36–38

I

intifada, 54
Iran-Iraq War, 54, 56
Islam, 9, 19, 22, 23–24, 25, 58, 59
Islamic Action Front, 58
Israel/Israelites, 6, 9, 11, 14, 15, 35, 38, 41–43, 45, 46, 48, 49, 53, 56, 56, 58

J

Jerusalem, 9, 14, 15, 24, 25, 39, 41, 43, 47, 49
  pilgrimage to, 20
Jews/Judaism, 9, 16, 18, 35, 38–40, 41
jihad, 29
Jordan
  location of, 6
  official name of, 5, 43
Judah, 14–15

K

kingdom, 12, 15
  of Israel, 14

L

language, 8
Lebanon, 36, 46
Levant, 14, 15, 23, 26, 28, 32

M

Mamluks, 26–28
McMahon Correspondence, 29, 32, 35
Mecca, 9, 22, 28, 29, 32, 38
Mongols, 26, 28
Muhammad, 9, 22, 23, 43
Muslim, 22, 29
  army, 22–23, 26
  capital, 24, 25
  civil war, 23

pilgrimage, 28
Shia, 23–24
Sunni, 23–24

N

Nabateans, 15–18, 58

P

Palestine, 6, 9, 10, 11, 15, 25, 28, 35, 36, 38–40, 43, 45, 46, 47, 48, 49, 51, 53, 54, 56
Palestine Liberation Organization (PLO), 47–49, 51, 53, 54–56
Persian Gulf War, 56
Philistines, 11

R

Roman Empire, 5, 16–19

S

Saladin (Salah ad-Din al-Ayyubi), 25, 26
Semites, 8–10, 12
Six-Day War, 46, 49
Stone Age, 7–8
Sykes-Picot Agreement, 32–35
Syria, 6, 10, 12, 15, 18, 22, 23, 25, 28, 35, 36, 43, 45, 46, 47, 49, 53, 54, 56, 58

T

Turks, 5, 15, 26, 32
  Ottoman, 28–29, 32
  Seljuk, 25

U

Umayyads, 5, 23–25
United Arab Republic (UAR), 45, 47
United Nations, 41, 45, 49

W

West Bank, 6, 7, 43, 49, 53, 54, 56

Z

Zionism, 38–39

About the Author

Amy Romano is the author of numerous magazine articles on a wide range of topics for national publications. Also the author of *A Historical Atlas of Afghanistan* and *A Historical Atlas of Israel* in the same series, Amy lives in Arizona with her husband, Don, and their children, Claudia, Sam, and Jack.

Acknowledgements

Special thanks to Karin van der Tak for her expert guidance regarding matters pertaining to the Middle East and Asia.

Photo Credits

Cover (map), pp. 1 (foreground), 4–5, 54–55 © 2002 Geoatlas; cover (background), pp. 1 (background), 14 Courtesy of the General Libraries, the University of Texas at Austin; cover (top left) © SEF/Art Resource, NY; cover (bottom left), p. 59 © AP/Wide World Photos; cover (bottom right), p. 19 © AKG London/Erich Lessing; p. 6 © Robert Holmes/Corbis; pp. 8, 24 (inset), 28 © Sonia Halliday Photographs/Jane Taylor; p. 9 © Archivo Iconografico, S.A./Corbis; pp. 10–11, 16 (top), 17, 22, 24, 32–33, 36–37, 42, 52–53, 57 maps designed by Tahara Hasan; pp. 12–13 © David Rubinger/Corbis; p. 16 (bottom) © Sonia Halliday Photographs; p. 18 © Scala/Art Resource, NY; pp. 20–21 © Stapleton Collection/Corbis; p. 25 © SEF/Art Resource, NY; pp. 26–27 © Historical Picture Archive/ Corbis; pp. 30–31 © Royalty-Free/Corbis; pp. 32, 38, 44, 48 © Bettmann/Corbis; p. 34 © Britain Israel Public Affairs Centre; pp. 40, 46 © Hulton/Archive/Getty Images; p. 50 © Maps.com/Corbis.

Designer: Tahara Hasan; **Editor:** Joann Jovinelly; **Photo Researcher:** Elizabeth Loving